Palm Springs

FIRST HUNDRED YEARS

FOR THE WOMEN IN MY LIFE

Negie, my wife

Donna, Cindy and Denni, my daughters

and Mary, my secretary

Palm Springs

FIRST HUNDRED YEARS

Frank M. Bogert
MAYOR OF PALM SPRINGS
1958 - 1966
1982 - 1988

REVISED AND UPDATED FROM THE 1987 EDITION
BY THE

PALM SPRINGS PUBLIC LIBRARY
Palm Springs, California
2003

LEFT: Frank Bogert in 1934
PHOTO BY DICK WHITTINGTON

First Edition 1987
Revised Edition with Epilogue 2003

Library of Congress Cataloging-in-Publication Data

Bogert, Frank M.
Palm Springs First Hundred Years / Frank M. Bogert. – Rev. and updated from the 1987 ed.
p. cm.
Includes index
ISBN 0-9618724-2-X
1. Palm Springs (Calif.)-History-Pictorial works. 2. Palm Springs (Calif.) – History. I. Title.

F869.P18B64 2003
979.4'97-dc21

2002193041

For information on this or any other Palm Springs Public Library publications, telephone 760 /323-8298, write to the Library Director at 300 South Sunrise Way, Palm Springs, CA 92262-7699, or visit the Library's web site at *www. PalmSpringsLibrary.org*

Graphic design by Clara Nelson, ClaraVoyant Design, Palm Springs, California
Printed in the United States of America by Crown Printers, Inc., San Bernardino, California

Contents

ABOVE: Two views of the Tennis Club swimming pool are seen in these hand-tinted post cards by Stephen Willard. This pool, also seen on the cover, is said to be the most photographed pool in Palm Springs.

PHOTOS BY STEPHEN WILLARD, PALM SPRINGS HISTORICAL SOCIETY COLLECTION

Frank M. Bogert

2002 Foreword

It was Margaret Roades, Palm Springs City Librarian, and Sally McManus, Curator of the Palm Springs Historical Society, who made this revision of *Palm Springs First Hundred Years* happen. It was their idea. They were the editors. They re-researched every fact and supervised the design and printing. They have my admiration, friendship and sincere thanks.

1987 Foreword

At best, this is but a thumbnail sketch of Palm Springs history – the first one hundred years. I leave it to a future chronicler to amass a more detailed report. In the meantime, hopefully this will help people understand how and why Palm Springs and the Coachella Valley became an internationally famed desert resort. My apologies are extended to the many people whom I do not mention, and to those whose photographs were impossible to reproduce for this book.

Sally McManus, Curator of the Palm Springs Historical Society, has worked diligently with me for three years, assisting with research and photograph requirements. Her enthusiastic attitude and vast knowledge have been invaluable.

Many other people have been unfailingly cooperative. I would particularly like to thank anthropologist Lowell Bean, Lena Lugo Martinez, Richard Milanovich and Katherine Siva Saubel for their help in securing information on the Agua Caliente Band of Cahuilla Indians. My thanks also to Milton Jones, publisher of *Palm Springs Life* magazine, for the use of his many color photographs and for his advice.

Suggestions and help of one kind or another were also graciously provided by Gil Grosvenor, President of the National Geographic Society; Mort Golden, Director of the Palm Springs Desert Museum; Elizabeth Coffman Kieley, President of the Palm Springs Historical Society; Gail Thompson; Jane Lykken Hoff; Jack Freeman; Ed McCoubrey; Virginia Marmolejo; Frank and John Miller; Ray Corliss; George Service; Yvonne Groggens; Nick Mutascio and many others too numerous to mention. Jack FitzGerald was particularly generous with his legal counsel and assistance. I am grateful to each of the fine photographers who shared generously from their archives and to my daughter, Donna Bogert Higueras, who created the title design.

Special thanks go to my ever-suffering secretary Mary Martin, who contacted many celebrities and corrected my mistakes; to Bob Wenkum, who did a masterful job of book design, layout and production in such a record time; and to Barbara Braasch, my editor, who made my words read so well.

F.M. Bogert

2002 Preface

Palm Springs in 1887 was the tiny oasis of Agua Caliente, already rich in the traditions of the Cahuilla Indians, but unknown to most of the world. Then, as now, this beautiful western end of the Coachella Valley was protected by the glorious Mt. San Jacinto, watered by the bubbling hot springs and bathed in the brilliant, golden light that can still be seen at special times of the morning and early evening.

The one hundred years that followed the arrival of John Guthrie McCallum as Indian Agent and first "landowner" were documented by former Palm Springs Mayor Frank M. Bogert in 1987. Mayor Bogert, who came to Palm Springs in 1927 to be a cowboy, participated in nearly every aspect of the development of Palm Springs. He became the public relations man for the El Mirador Hotel early in his colorful career and began using his camera for publicity shots of celebrities and wealthy winter visitors. He captured fascinating photographs, collected them, and, throughout his life, has been the subject of many. Some of the best of his photographs and many others were compiled into this remarkable book, along with a narrative describing the growth of Palm Springs from oasis to village to world-famous resort city, as Mr. Bogert lived it. *Palm Springs First Hundred Years* became one of the most compelling histories of this fabulous city and sold out all copies many years ago. The Board of Trustees of the Palm Springs Public Library, with Mayor Bogert's permission and assistance, is privileged to offer this revised edition.

The former mayor is a much-loved and honored figure in Palm Springs, and his book will be used as a historical resource for many years to come. It has been an honor and joy to work with him and his great, good friend Ray Corliss to ensure that it retained its original flavor throughout editing. They have approved of, and usually enhanced, every change, and it is still very much "Frank's book."

In general, the original chapters have been corrected to reflect deaths and other changes. The spelling of names was rigorously checked. Buildings or places that no longer exist or have had major renovations and name changes have been given location references. Facts regarding such events as the building of the Aerial Tramway and a very few incorrect captions have been reviewed and revised where necessary. Because Chapter Six, "The Valley Today," written in 1987, would have been misleading to a new reader, an epilogue has been added to summarize major changes that have occurred in the Coachella Valley through 2001. The title remains the same, however: *Palm Springs First Hundred Fifteen Years* simply does not have the right resonance!

The Board of Library Trustees and the editors wish to thank Mayor Bogert and Mr. Corliss for their assistance, unflagging good cheer, and remarkable stories, many of which, sadly, are unlikely to ever make it to any book. The Library's reference staff has been resourceful and wonderful, as has Assistant City Librarian Josette McNary. The archives of the Palm Springs Historical Society have been invaluable, and we are grateful for the patience of the Historical Society Board. Clara Nelson's artistic talents and good sense have kept the book on track. Deepest thanks are due to photographers Tom Brewster, Arthur Coleman, Kirk Owens and George Service; and to the Palm Springs Desert Resorts Convention and Visitors Authority for its photo resources. Many others helped to verify facts and offer assistance: Dan Callahan, Kitty Kieley Hayes, Jane Lykken Hoff, Andy Hollinger, Tom and Elizabeth Kieley, Mayor William G. Kleindienst, Clarence Macy, Margot Martin, Virginia Mendoza, Scott Mikesell, Richard Milanovich, the late Earl Neel, Jade Nelson, Steve Nichols, Jean Penn, Jamie Lee Pricer, Marvin Roos, John Sanborn, Julius Shulman, Alvino Siva and Suzanne Sutton.

The Board of Library Trustees is deeply grateful, in addition, to the generous benefactors who understood the importance of preserving this significant history and helped to underwrite the costs of making it available once again. They were Jim and Jackie Lee Houston, the Agua Caliente Band of Cahuilla Indians Tribal Council, Mrs. Gene Autry, the Friends of the Palm Springs Library, the Joseph P. Koss Memorial Fund and the Palm Springs Preservation Foundation.

Margaret Roades
Palm Springs City Librarian

Sally McManus
Director, Palm Springs Historical Society

To Frank -
The only
Mayor in P.S.
Forever
Best
For Frank
Happy memories
Dolores Hope

Good Wishes From
BOB HOPE

I love Palm Springs. It's the only city that doesn't think Johnny Carson gets enough time off.

I've been going to Palm Springs off and on for the past fifty years and every time I looked up Frank Bogert was mayor again. And I've never missed seeing him around there – even during the days of the "ChiChi" and "The Desert Inn". He was always doing something for the community and he's never stopped.

Yeah, Frank's been here a long time. When he started, there was nothing here but a few gophers and Charlie Farrell.

In those days there was no Aerial Tramway – nothing – the highest thing there was, was Phil Harris – and it still is.

Frank has served us in many ways. He was in the Navy as a lieutenant commander. He was in charge of a battleship which later turned out to be a submarine. There's no way I could account for all of his municipal jobs – he's been on so many commissions, luring the tourists, President of the Desert Circus, the Museum, Rodeo, and he'll even come over and do the lawn. And he does all that and still finds time to play golf.

Palm Springs is the winter golf capital of the world. You have to shoot par to get a room down here. And it's on account of the weather. It's always so great. The Palm Springs weather man is a recording. It's also one of the healthiest places in the world.

And they're making progress and bringing culture to Palm Springs. The other day I saw a lizard wearing a tuxedo.

Frank Bogert has lived through all of it. The man is a great public servant. A man of integrity, honesty and absolutely incorruptible. How he got the job in the first place I'll never know.

He's a great family man. He has a flock of grandchildren and they get along well because he speaks their language. He spent the past year as a member of the President's Commission of Americans Outdoors. He belonged with the group because he's helped keep Palm Springs great for the past fifty years.

Bob Hope

1987

Introduction

One hundred years ago only the Agua Caliente Band of Cahuilla Indians lived in what is now known as Palm Springs.

PREVIOUS PAGES: Cahuilla basketmakers in 1898. Pedro Chino stands in the doorway of his home and his wife Marie works on a large basket that would now be highly valued by collectors and museums.

PALM SPRINGS HISTORICAL SOCIETY COLLECTION

LEFT: The wives and daughters of three of the Patencio brothers. From the left: Dolores, wife of Francisco Patencio; Celia, daughter of Moreno Patencio; and the daughters and wife of Albert Patencio – Florita, Matilda and Colastica. Florita (Flora) Patencio Cruz lived in Palm Springs all of her life.

PALM SPRINGS DESERT MUSEUM COLLECTION

In the late 1800s, settlers looking for a dry, healthy climate were attracted to the desert by developers' brochures. They cleared the land of creosote bushes and cactus, constructed irrigation canals, planted crops and created a village.

An 1887 brochure advertising the wonders of Palm Valley.

COURTESY SEAVER CENTER FOR WESTERN HISTORY RESEARCH
NATURAL HISTORY MUSEUM OF LOS ANGELES COUNTY

By train and automobile, new residents arrived to populate the desert and enjoy the hot springs. Sanatoriums became hotels, and as the valley resort became popular, the village grew into a city that was incorporated in 1938.

A great tourist attraction in the 1920s, Palm Canyon gained fame from the books of George Wharton James and William Strong, the paintings of Carl Eytel and Jimmy Swinnerton, and the photography of William Lockwood and Stephen Willard. The photo taken at Hermit's Bench in Palm Canyon in 1927 shows Sunday drivers on a typical desert afternoon.

PALM SPRINGS HISTORICAL SOCIETY COLLECTION

1929 brochure from the El Mirador Hotel

As filmmakers discovered the pleasant climate, Hollywood celebrities arrived with photographers, writers and artists who told the world about Palm Springs as an unsurpassed vacation destination.

ABOVE: Early cinematographers shoot the action of a stagecoach from a flatbed truck against a backdrop of the Mt. San Jacinto foothills.

RIGHT: *Peer Gynt* is the earliest known film made in Palm Springs, circa 1916. It was a silent adaptation of the play starring Cyril Maude and Alma Rubens.

PALM SPRINGS HISTORICAL SOCIETY COLLECTION

The Coachella Valley and Palm Springs became an international playground with golf courses, tennis courts and winter horseback riding. A year-round tramway takes visitors from the desert floor to the mountains.

Palm Springs is a world-renowned resort and the proud address for major hotels, international shops, restaurants and thousands of permanent residents. This sophisticated city still embraces village friendliness and desert amenities that have contributed to its growth over the past hundred years.

PREVIOUS PAGES: Golfers enjoy the morning sun and lush fairways of Mesquite Country Club. Mt. San Jacinto rises in the background.

RIGHT: The inviting pool area of the Wyndham Hotel – Palm Springs shimmers like a jewel at dusk.

PHOTOS BY TOM BREWSTER

1

An Indian Beginning

According to anthropologists, Native Americans have lived beside the sparkling waters of Palm Springs' tree-lined canyons and around its bubbling hot springs for over a thousand years. They survived by using a multitude of desert plants for food, clothing and medicine. With bows and arrows and sticks, the Indians hunted deer, bighorn sheep, rabbits and other small animals. Recent discoveries indicate that their irrigation ditches may date back to pre-Columbian time.

After the arrival of the Spaniards, the Indians grew corn, squash, beans and melons. They later cultivated orchards and began raising cattle and horses.

The Agua Caliente Indians of Palm Springs are one of ten or more independent clans of the Cahuilla tribe from the Shoshonean division *(Takic)* of the Uto-Aztecan language family. Their traditional communities were located in Palm, Andreas, Murray, Tahquitz and Chino canyons.

Closely allied with the Cahuilla clans of the Indian Wells and San Gorgonio Pass areas, the Agua Calientes also maintained social, religious and economic relationships with Indians from Los Angeles to the Colorado River. The Cahuillas all spoke the same language with some dialectical variations, a language closely related to their Serrano, Gabrieliño and Luiseño neighbors.

The Cahuillas had clan-based sovereignty over particular desert and mountain territories. Each community supervised specific areas used by its people for gathering food, hunting, ritual observances and recreation. Disputes in Cahuilla history were usually over hunting and food-gathering boundaries.

Chief Cabezon, who lived in the Thermal-Mecca region, was recognized as a leader, or *Cacique,* by many of the Cahuillas and was given considerable authority by the Mexicans and Americans. His nominal control extended over Indians from the desert through the San Gorgonio Pass. After his death, his son continued to exercise power over the tribe until his own death in the late nineteenth century.

LEFT: Palm Canyon, with more than two thousand palms, is the largest of the canyons. The lower part of the canyon is owned by the Agua Caliente Indians. Riding and hiking trails extend for miles into the canyon's upper reaches.

PHOTO BY KIRK OWENS

An Agua Caliente family portrait of three generations: Juan Bautista Lugo and his wife Apolinaria, their two daughters, Margarita and Romalda, and Romalda's daughter, Lorena (Lena). Lugo, from the village of Cahuilla, was raised by the Franciscan Fathers at the Santa Barbara Mission, where he learned to speak fluent Spanish. He left the mission when he was eighteen and settled in Hemet and Anza, where he worked as a sheepshearer and married Apolinaria, who then lived at Agua Caliente.

PHOTO COURTESY LENA LUGO MARTINEZ

Other famous Cahuilla leaders included Juan Antonio, later appointed a general by General Stephen Kearney and a captain general by the Superintendent of Indian Affairs in 1855, and Antonio Garra, an authoritative figure in the 1840s. Like Cabezon, they both functioned as intermediaries between the confederated Cahuilla groups and early pioneers entering the region.

All Cahuilla people belonged to one of two social groups – the wild cat, *Istam*, or the coyote, *Tuktum*. These moieties were subdivided into a large number of clans. Membership into a clan was through the father; members of *Istam* were expected to marry into the *Tuktum* clan and vice versa.

By the turn of the century, Agua Caliente (as Palm Springs was called in the 1800s) became a focus of Cahuilla activity. The *Paniktum* lineage of Andreas Canyon was closely related to the *Kauisiktum* lineage of Agua Caliente and joined them in ceremonies, along with other groups which no longer had a ceremonial leader.

Alejo Patencio was the *Net*, or head man, of the *Kauisiktum* clan in 1925. This was an office that passed from father to son unless the son was not qualified, in which case it reverted to another member of the family. The *Net* administered the affairs of his clan and settled disputes. His word was final and respected. He knew all the clan songs and legendary history as well as the minute landmarks of the clan's territory and food-gathering areas. He set the dates for all ceremonies and told his people when it was time to gather their various crops.

The *Net* ruled his domain from the roundhouse, or *Kishumnawut*, in Section 14 (of the reservation land) of Palm Springs. Considered a sacred site, it was the location of ceremonial dances and the place where the clan members kept the *Maiswat*, their sacred belongings.

Marcus Belardo was Alejo Patencio's *Paxaa*, an assistant with special duties. His responsibilities included keeping order and silence at all solemn ceremonies, collecting food from each family for the roundhouse ceremonies, and overseeing ceremonial protocol. This respected office, like the *Net*, passed from father to son.

Other clan officers included the *Takwa*, who prepared and distributed the food at ceremonies, and the *Haunik*, who sang at all the functions. The *Haunik* was revered by the clan for his fine voice and his repertoire of poetic song cycles, some of which lasted as long as twelve hours. He taught tribal history and songs to the young people and instructed them in proper adult behavior. Joe Patencio was the last person to hold this office.

The shamans, or medicine men, were called *Puvalem*. The *Pavuul* exerted greater power than the *Puul*, the less-revered shamans. Pedro Chino was a *Pavuul* noted for his extraordinary powers for predicting future events, making rain, stopping catastrophes and other "miracles." He supposedly could change into a crow, mountain lion, coyote or other bird or animal.

Juan Bautista Lugo and Apolinaria in their later years.
PHOTO COURTESY LENA LUGO MARTINEZ

Puvalem were highly respected clan members. It was thought that they could cure any ailment with their considerable knowledge of herbs and other medical procedures and neutralize the power of evil spirits with special songs and dances. They were an important part of all ceremonies and advised the *Net* of the most propitious time for all events. To demonstrate their power, they performed extraordinary feats such as eating hot coals at ceremonies.

Puvalem did not inherit their office, but were born with their powers or taught by *Puul* who recognized a youth's talent. Often, both the *Net* and the *Paxaa* were *Puvalem*. These ceremonial roles and duties were quite confusing to pioneers, who mistakenly assumed all the participants to be chiefs.

This photograph taken in 1898 in front of Pedro Chino's house *(kish)* shows Agua Caliente women weaving baskets, considered to be among the best in the country. Many Indians from Torres-Martinez and other bands came to Agua Caliente for the desired weaving materials and hot water.
PALM SPRINGS HISTORICAL SOCIETY COLLECTION

In later years, the Agua Calientes also elected a secular leader to act as liaison between the clan and governmental agencies and other outside groups. His powers were limited and had no connection with the ceremonies. Lee Arenas, one of the best known of the clan leaders, often acted as a guide and interpreter for the area's white settlers. He later led the fight to have reservation land allotted to individual members of the tribe. Today, the Agua Caliente people have an elected council to administer tribal affairs.

At the beginning of the twentieth century, many of the Cahuillas spoke Spanish and had Spanish names, but, thanks to their remote location, they were able to escape much Mexican influence and to preserve most of their Indian culture.

The Americanization of the Indians began after the Mormons settled in San Bernardino around 1852. Soon, their influence extended as far south as San Timoteo Canyon, with several settlers moving into the San Gorgonio Pass region. By 1862, the Bradshaw Trail ran from Redlands to Arizona, and Agua Caliente became an important stage stop and a one-day trip from Banning.

Jack Summers ran the way station and raised barley for horses on ten acres he rented from the Indians. Many Agua Calientes got jobs on the railroad Southern Pacific built through the pass in 1875. The Craft family had a large orchard near Yucaipa and hired many Indians. Among them was Francisco Patencio, an excellent farmer. Pedro Chino and Miguel Saturnino, both highly-skilled cowpunchers, went to work for Paulino Weaver, who ran four thousand head of cattle on his ranch in San Gorgonio Pass.

The number of Agua Calientes began to diminish in later years. Because of their close association with white people, many Indians fell victim to the great smallpox epidemic of 1862. By 1884, around seventy Indians were living in the Palm Springs area; in 1925, only fifty remained. Today *[1987]* the tribe numbers two hundred forty members. *[Eds. Note: As of 2001, tribal members number three hundred seventy-seven.]*

Fortunately, David Prescott Barrows arrived on the scene in 1900 to prepare an anthropological report on Cahuilla culture. By the early 1920s Alfred Kroeber, Lucille Hooper and William Duncan Strong had studied and published material on the Cahuillas. In 1972, Dr. Lowell Bean published one of the best anthropological studies of an Indian tribe: *Mukat's People* was based on his fifteen years of work with the Cahuilla elders and members of the tribe.

After reading Bean's book, one cannot help but have a tremendous admiration for these interesting people. They are a strong, intelligent, tenacious group with a high degree of morality and integrity. That they could exist in such a barren environment shows considerable initiative and great industry.

The Cahuillas' oral treasures are highly poetic and their crafts were extremely artistic in design. All of their tools, mats, baskets and pottery show a high order of craftsmanship. Many of today's young Cahuillas have rediscovered their culture and are rightfully proud of their heritage.

Unidentified Agua Caliente basketmaker.

PALM SPRINGS HISTORICAL SOCIETY COLLECTION

Early resident Pedro Chino often talked of a hot spring in Chino Canyon with special curative waters. In 1932, Culver Nichols, owner of the Chino Canyon oasis, rediscovered the hot spring where it had been covered with debris and vines. The last thatched Indian house was still there in 1911 and might have been where Carl Eytel stayed while sketching and painting in the canyon.

PHOTO COURTESY SHEILA GRATTAN, PALM SPRINGS DESERT MUSEUM COLLECTION

RIGHT: Lee Arenas, shown with his wife Guadalupe and adopted daughter Della, was one of the best known of the Agua Calientes. Famed for his prowess as a runner, Arenas won everything from the hundred-yard dash to a twelve-mile foot race. He was the Agua Caliente elected leader for dealing with government agencies and white settlers. The Arenas family is shown with two staple foods, mesquite beans and a jack rabbit, used by the Indian people then living in the desert valley.

PHOTO BY J. SMEATON CHASE, FRANK BOGERT COLLECTION

Chief Cabezon, son of a very influential officer appointed by the Mexicans during their California reign, was given papers that granted him nominal control over all the Cahuillas and Serranos from the desert through San Gorgonio Pass. When he died in 1883, reportedly at the age of 120, his authority passed to his son, who remained a very important chief until his death in 1887. Their village was north of Coachella, where the present day Cabazon Reservation is located.

PHOTO COURTESY ANTHONY ANDREAS, JR.

Julian Augustine and his two daughters, Augusta and Margaret, from the Augustine Reservation near Coachella, pose in a photographer's studio about 1900.

PHOTO COURTESY ANTHONY ANDREAS, JR.

RIGHT: John Joseph Andreas and his wife Margaret Augustine Andreas were photographed in 1910, the year of their marriage. Andreas was the grandfather of Anthony Andreas, Jr., a former historian of the Agua Caliente Band.

PHOTO COURTESY ANTHONY ANDREAS, JR.

ABOVE: A group of Cahuilla children photographed about 1910.

PALM SPRINGS HISTORICAL SOCIETY COLLECTION

BELOW: The peon game, a complicated gambling game that uses pieces of bone, is still popular among Indians throughout Southern California at fiestas, powwows and social events, with one reservation usually playing against another. In this photo, probably taken around 1900, the stakes were beads, baskets, stone sharpeners, pots and tools. Today, the stakes are cash. Each person on the four-member team has two bones made from a coyote shin bone – one black, the other white. Each bone has a string attached, tying the bone to the player's wrist. Sitting down facing each other, the playing teams cover their hands with a blanket, holding a bone in each hand. When ready, the referee, called a *coyme*, gives the word to begin and the first player on the opposing team guesses in which hand each player holds the white bone. For every incorrect guess the *coyme* places a stick on the ground next to that team. When a team counts fifteen sticks beside them, the other team is the winner. Each team has its own traditional songs and women join in the singing throughout the game.

PHOTO COURTESY ANTHONY ANDREAS, JR.

LEFT: The Cahuillas made beautiful ollas of clay by the coil method. They used the ollas to store grain and seeds. This olla was discovered and photographed by J. Smeaton Chase in Andreas Canyon in 1911. The ollas usually were found in inaccessible places, covered with palm fibers and rocks.

FRANK BOGERT COLLECTION

BELOW: Dolores Patencio, a Cupeño basketmaker, was married to Francisco Patencio, one of the last ceremonial leaders of the Agua Calientes. Their grandnephew, Ray Patencio, was a past chairman and secretary of the tribal council.

PHOTO BY HANNAHS,
GAIL THOMPSON COLLECTION

ABOVE: Marcus Belardo was the second ceremonial chief, *Paxaa*, of the Agua Calientes and assisted the *Net*, head man of the village, in all ceremonies. Belardo was responsible for keeping silence and order as well as making announcements and singing appropriately. At one time he owned his own date orchard and considered his profession to be date farmer. Indian agent and farming instructor Adrian Maxwell's son, Kermit, is shown here with Marcus in 1916.

PALM SPRINGS DESERT MUSEUM COLLECTION

ABOVE: Rosie and Marcus Belardo about 1920, at the annual Palm Springs Easter sunrise services, always held on the hill behind The Desert Inn. The Belardos were a well-known and popular couple with the early white settlers of Palm Springs.

PALM SPRINGS DESERT MUSEUM COLLECTION

ABOVE: Miss Cornelia White *(second from left)* was an avid explorer, riding and hiking to all parts of the Coachella Valley. White is shown here with Agua Caliente Indians who often accompanied her as guides. Brothers Lee and Simon Arenas are at the far right, the others are unidentified.

PALM SPRINGS DESERT MUSEUM COLLECTION

LEFT: Romalda Lugo, daughter Lena, and their dog Negro were photographed in 1913. Lena Lugo Martinez has lived in Palm Springs all her life, where she has been an outspoken leader of the Agua Calientes. Her childhood memories have been invaluable to ethnologists collecting information about the desert Indians.

PHOTO COURTESY LENA MARTINEZ

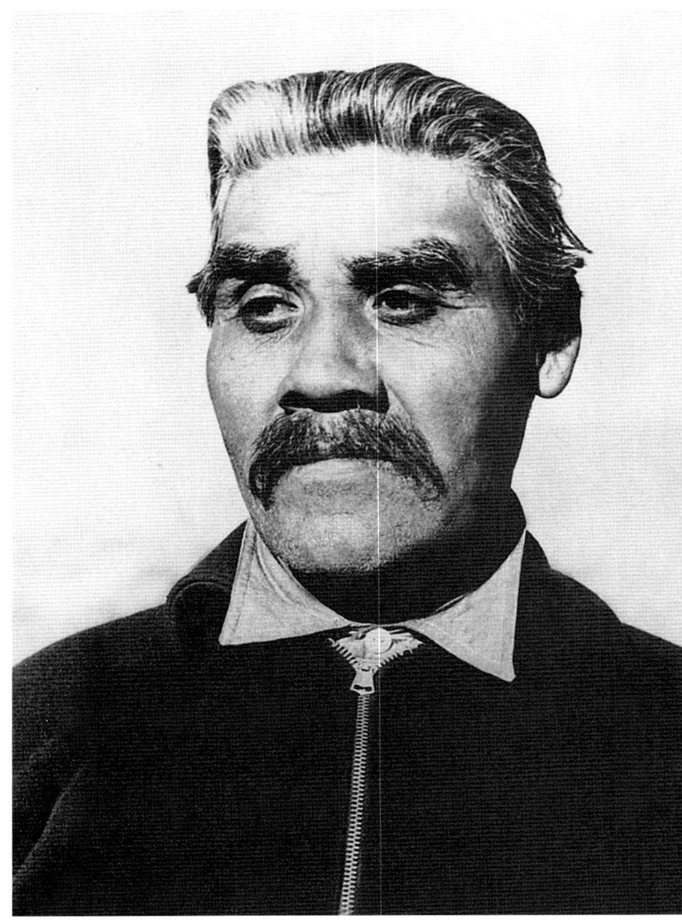

ABOVE: John Andreas was born on the Craft ranch between Banning and Redlands, where many of the local Indians worked during the harvesting season. Andreas' Palm Springs home was in the village of Rincon just below the mouth of Andreas Canyon, where the *Paniktum* clan lived. Indians living in Section 14 around the hot springs were called the *Kauisiktum* clan.

PHOTO COURTESY ANTHONY ANDREAS, JR.

ABOVE: Frank Bogert took this photo of Pedro Chino in 1934, when Chino was said to be 113 years old, but Indian records showed him to be nearer 95. Chino was a *Puvalem*, a medicine man, born with special healing powers and respected by all the Cahuillas. As a youth, he punched cattle on Paulino Weaver's ranch in the San Gorgonio Pass and was an excellent horseman, with horses and cattle of his own. When he died in 1939, Indians from all over Southern California attended his funeral.

PHOTO BY FRANK BOGERT, PALM SPRINGS HISTORICAL SOCIETY COLLECTION

BELOW AND FACING PAGE: An 1898 funeral procession to the Indian cemetery, now known as the Jane Augustine Patencio Cemetery, located on Tahquitz Canyon Drive. The gentleman in the long coat and beard *(at far left on facing page)* is Welwood Murray, who looks on as coffin is lowered into the ground. Those in attendance pass by and drop a handful of earth into the grave, after which the pallbearers fill the grave and erect the cross.

PALM SPRINGS HISTORICAL SOCIETY COLLECTION

An aristocratic Calistro Lugo poses for photographer Val Samuelson. Lugo, the son of itinerant farm workers, was orphaned at an early age and reared by Henry and Margarita Pablo on the Morongo Reservation. After the death of his adoptive parents, Lugo moved to Palm Springs to live out his years with Margarita Pablo's sister, Romalda Lugo Taylor.

PALM SPRINGS HISTORICAL SOCIETY COLLECTION

By 1939 Clemente Segundo managed the Indian bathhouse on Section 14 in Palm Springs. The bathhouse not only welcomed tourists, but also local Indians and white settlers. The price was twenty-five cents – towel not included. The corners of four rooms intersected over the spring. As the water slowly washed beneath their feet, bathers could immerse themselves completely, sometimes contacting legs dangling down from adjacent rooms. The water temperature was about 104 degrees, with a decidedly sulphuric smell and a considerable reputation for curative powers.

PALM SPRINGS HISTORICAL SOCIETY COLLECTION

ABOVE: As late as 1915, most of the Indian houses were on Section 14 in Palm Springs. The homes were made of wood and palm fronds, some with special roofs made of shakes brought in by white settlers. Before the arrival of the white pioneers, Indians constructed their homes from various local plant materials. Palm fronds were ideal for thatched roofs. Pitched roofs and adobe walls were added after the first mission church was built. (The church, then St. Florian's, is now Our Lady of Guadalupe on the corner of East Arenas Road and Calle El Segundo.)

PALM SPRINGS HISTORICAL SOCIETY COLLECTION

RIGHT: Desert Indians had to be constantly on guard to protect their crops of corn, squash, watermelons, tomatoes, cantaloupes and alfalfa from stray cattle, marauding animals and occasional visits from neighborhood kids looking for watermelons. A shady ramada constructed of local foliage made the guard work considerably more comfortable.

PALM SPRINGS HISTORICAL SOCIETY COLLECTION

LEFT: Miguel Saturnino was an Agua Caliente cattleman. As a youth, he learned the ranching business on Paulino Weaver's ranch in the San Gorgonio Pass. In 1910, when he was photographed by J. Smeaton Chase, he owned a large herd of cattle which he ranged in the Palm Springs area. His grandnephew is Richard Milanovich, current Tribal Chairman.

FRANK BOGERT COLLECTION

A local resident demonstrates how the Indians cut out the heart of the agave plant which was then baked on an open fire, covered with leaves and left overnight in the hot coals. The agave, tasting very much like a yam, was a staple of the desert Indian diet.

PHOTO TAKEN IN 1916 BY J. SMEATON CHASE, FRANK BOGERT COLLECTION

At the turn of the twentieth century local Indians were still living in homes made from native materials. This photo was taken in Section 14, where most of the Indians lived, within a short walk to the bathhouse, the ceremonial house, St. Florian's Church and the graveyard.

PALM SPRINGS HISTORICAL SOCIETY COLLECTION

ABOVE: Lee Arenas and his brother Simon make fire by rubbing sticks together in Palm Canyon.
FRANK BOGERT COLLECTION

RIGHT: The town of Indian Wells was named for the wells in the area. Excavated from the valley floor, they were important water sources for Indians. Today the open shafts have been filled and can no longer be found. The Cahuillas dug as deep as thirty feet, with steps going down to the water surface.
GAIL THOMPSON COLLECTION

ABOVE: Lee Arenas in the Santa Rosa Mountains, 1911

PHOTO BY J. SMEATON CHASE, FRANK BOGERT COLLECTION

RIGHT: A very distinguished tribal member, Lee Arenas, shortly before his death in 1966 at the age of 98. Arenas had fought for many years to have the thirty-two thousand acre Agua Caliente Reservation divided among the individual members of the Band. The Mission Indian Relief Act of 1891 gave the Secretary of the Interior authority to make such allotments, but the Secretary refused to do so. Lee was firmly convinced of the Indians' right to their land and over many years pleaded for action in every court available to him, finally winning his case before the U.S. Supreme Court in 1944. The Indians finally owned their own land. Most Indians were allotted forty-seven acres – two acres in town in the west half of Section 14, five acres in the east portion for irrigated farm land, and forty acres outside Section 14 in alternating sections scattered across the valley. President Dwight D. Eisenhower signed an equalization bill in 1959 that gave every member of the Band allotments with an equal value of no less than $335,000.

PHOTO BY GAIL THOMPSON

RIGHT: Lee Arenas and his second wife, the former Marian Scott, stroll in front of their Orchard Trailer Park. Marian, a Luiseño from the Pala Reservation near Temecula, was beautiful, intelligent and well-educated. She died in 1982.

PHOTO BY GAIL THOMPSON

STOP

ABOVE: Tollkeeper John Joseph Andreas in front of the tollbooth at the entrance to Andreas, Palm and Murray canyons about 1938. Today, the beautiful, unspoiled canyons are still a source of pleasure to hikers, tourists and local residents.

PHOTO COURTESY ANTHONY ANDREAS, JR.

LEFT: Francisco Patencio and wife Dolores. Francisco, along with his brothers, Alejo, Moreno and Albert, were leaders of the clan. Francisco became the best known of the brothers, as he was a teller of Indian legends and stories. These were published in 1943 by Margaret Boynton. Dolores, of the Cupeño band, originally from the Warner Ranch, was one of the most famous basketmakers in the Palm Springs area.

PHOTO TAKEN IN 1928 BY HANNAHS, GAIL THOMPSON COLLECTION

Celia Patencio, sister of the last ceremonial singer, Joseph Patencio. He knew all the Indian bird songs and the song of the history of creation, the latter taking twelve hours to sing. Celia was married to Harry Hopkins, the grandson of the legendary Ramona.

PHOTO COURTESY ANTHONY ANDREAS, JR.

ABOVE: One of the best-known Cahuillas in the valley was Fig Tree John, who usually donned his army uniform and high silk hat to greet visitors. His real name was Juanito Razon; Fig Tree was derived from the many fig trees planted around his home. When he died in 1927, his son claimed he was 136 years old.

PHOTO BY C.C. PIERCE, FRANK BOGERT COLLECTION

BELOW: Fig Tree John posed for desert author-photographer J. Smeaton Chase about 1918 in front of his home at Agua Dulce on the west bank of the Salton Sea. In his book, *Our Araby*, Chase writes "good camping places by the sea with fair water, are at Fig Tree John Springs and Fish Springs."

PALM SPRINGS HISTORICAL SOCIETY COLLECTION

ABOVE: Photograph taken in 1915 in front of Adrian Maxwell's house on Indian Avenue, present day site of the Spa Hotel. TOP ROW, LEFT TO RIGHT: Adrian Maxwell, Indian farm instructor and agent, Amado Miguel, Maxwell's wife Alice, Lee Arenas, Gabe Costa, Clemente Segundo, John Segundo, Pedro Chino, Tom Segundo, Francisco Arenas, an unidentified man, and Marcus Belardo. BOTTOM ROW: Kermit Maxwell, Augusta Patencio, Ellen Maxwell, Mrs. Pedro (Marie) Chino, Mrs. Francisco (Dolores) Patencio, Emma Pete, Mrs. Lee (Lupe) Arenas, little Della Arenas, and Mrs. Marcus (Rosie) Belardo.

PHOTO BY J. SMEATON CHASE, FRANK BOGERT COLLECTION

Indian police in Andreas Canyon. Leaning against the rock is Will Pablo of the Morongo Reservation. Pablo was responsible for bringing Judge John Guthrie McCallum to Palm Springs in 1884, and he was nominal chief under Captain Cabezon.

FRANK BOGERT COLLECTION

ABOVE: A.B. Trott, a guest at Welwood Murray's hotel, posed Pedro Chino and his wife Marie in front of their home in 1898. During these years, Pedro, an excellent horseman, was a cowboy on Paulino Weaver's ranch in the San Gorgonio Pass. He later became an important tribal medicine man.

PALM SPRINGS HISTORICAL SOCIETY COLLECTION

Young descendants of some well-known pioneers in Palm Springs pose in the late 1970s at a benefit for Our Lady of Solitude Catholic Church where they demonstrated a Cahuilla Bird Dance as part of the entertainment. TOP ROW, LEFT TO RIGHT: Eugene Pablo, Matt Pablo (son of Will Pablo), and brothers Anthony and John Andreas. MIDDLE ROW: Paula Andreas, Anna Patencio, Cheryl Rae Andreas, Ronette Saubel, Lorena Saubel, and Leila Saubel. BOTTOM ROW, KNEELING: Leonard Saubel, Jr. and Delbert Saubel, Jr.

ANTHONY ANDREAS COLLECTION

LEFT: Francisco Patencio in front of the ceremonial roundhouse. Patencio was the ceremonial chief of the Agua Calientes – the *Net*. Made of palm fronds, the house was called *Kishumnawut* by the Cahuillas. The *Maiswut*, or sacred bundle, was kept here. It was also the home of the *Net*, or head man of the village. Dances and important ceremonies were held in this sacred building. When the last *Net* died, the *Kishumnawut* was burned down and the *Maiswut* and sacred shell beads buried with him.

PALM SPRINGS DESERT MUSEUM COLLECTION

2

Challenging the Environment

While the Californias were being explored over the course of two centuries, the Palm Springs area remained undiscovered by white pioneers until 1823. In that year, Captain Jose Romero led an expedition through the San Gorgonio Pass in search of a route to the Colorado River. His party stopped to rest at some natural hot springs, which they named Agua Caliente.

Just over twenty years later, in 1845, B.D. Wilson was directed by Pio Pico, Mexico's last California governor, to lead a posse into the area in pursuit of a couple of renegade Indians. Wilson and his sixty men met with Cahuilla Chief Cabezon, who handed the renegades over to them at Agua Caliente.

Eight years later, W.P. Blake, a geologist with the Smithsonian Institution, was sent by the Federal government to survey land across the west for a possible railroad route from the Mississippi to the Pacific. In his detailed report, Blake described the palm-shaded mineral pool and the friendly Indians of Agua Caliente who lived by the hot springs that fed into it.

Few visited the area, however, until transportation became more available after California acquired statehood in 1850. Various stagecoaches and freight lines crossed the desert during the 1850s and 1860s, the most interesting of which was operated by "Big Bill Bradshaw." He chose the oasis as a stopping point for his stage, which ran along the Bradshaw Trail from Los Angeles to the gold fields of Arizona.

Bradshaw built a stage stop and called it "Agua Caliente." It was the first time that the name Agua Caliente was used for the oasis. Jack Summers, hired to operate the station, became the area's first non-Indian settler. The adobe hut in which Summers lived from 1862 to 1876 remained standing until the early 1920s.

Ironically, San Gorgonio Pass, the easiest and most logical entrance into the Los Angeles basin from the east, was for many years unknown to early pioneers who spilled blood, sweat, and tears to reach their final destination along dangerous and much more difficult routes.

LEFT: Early settlers had to deal with the harsh local environment. Rocks, sand, water supply and extreme weather conditions were among the environmental challenges they dealt with. Thankfully, the natural beauty and climate were incentive for them to persist and settle in Palm Springs.

PHOTO BY GEORGE SERVICE

PREVIOUS PAGES: Aerial view of Palm Springs and Mt. San Jacinto taken around 1930. The San Gorgonio Pass and Mt. San Gorgonio are on the right.

PHOTO COURTESY GEORGE VALEUR

An 1886 photo of Indian Avenue, now Indian Canyon Drive, Palm Springs' second major street and the location of major hotels and businesses.
PALM SPRINGS DESERT MUSEUM COLLECTION

The railroad finally made it through the pass in 1876. However, Agua Caliente was still very remote and few people knew of its existence. For ten miles on either side of the tracks, the land was divided by the government into a checkerboard pattern. Southern Pacific Railroad received odd-numbered sections while the even-numbered ones remained government property. Many years later, forty-eight sections were given to the Agua Caliente Band of Cahuilla Indians.

Pedro Chino sold ten acres of his land, located between the hot spring and mountain, known since as Chino Canyon, to two white men in 1880, long before the land boom began. Though the land belonged to the railroad and was not his to sell, old Chino, who had lived there for years, figured he had the right to sell it. The two men, W. E. Van Slyke and M. Byrne, bought still more land from the railroad and formed the Palm City Water Company.

Palm Springs wouldn't be what it is today without the influence of John Guthrie McCallum, the first non-Indian to settle permanently in the tiny oasis known as Agua Caliente. McCallum, a San Francisco lawyer, had moved to San Bernardino as agent for the Mission Indian Agency in 1883. McCallum's interpreter at the time was Will Pablo, a Cahuilla Indian from the Morongo Reservation, who introduced him to Agua Caliente's hot springs and benign desert climate. In 1885, McCallum resigned his position and moved his family to the unofficially renamed Palm City hoping that the warm, dry desert climate would improve the health of his young son, John, who was suffering from tuberculosis.

Section 14 of the city's checkerboard pattern contained the hot springs. McCallum bought a one-fifth interest in the bordering sections of 13, 15, 23 and 25, and a one-fifth interest in the Palm City Water Company. The deed was signed March 24, 1885.

That same year, the local Indian band, which numbered around seventy-six, helped the McCallums build an adobe house on what is now West Tahquitz Canyon Way between Belardo Road and South Palm Canyon Drive. The house was later moved to its present site, the Village Green on South Palm Canyon Drive, and is headquarters for the Palm Springs Historical Society.

Judge John G. McCallum with his wife Emily and son Harry McCallum at their Los Angeles home.

PALM SPRINGS HISTORICAL SOCIETY COLLECTION

Emily McCallum had borne six children, but one had died in infancy and three others at early ages. Wallace died in 1896 at the age of 30 from heart disease aggravated by alcoholism; Harry died in 1901, also at the age of 30, from pulmonary tuberculosis; and May died from typhoid when she was in her late thirties. Although Johnny McCallum almost regained his health, he contracted pneumonia which reactivated the tuberculosis. On a trip to San Diego to seek relief, he became ill and died at the Hotel Del Coronado at the age of 26. Pearl was the McCallum's only surviving child.

McCallum had a dream. He thought the region could become a major agricultural center where, because of the early growing season, crops could be shipped to Los Angeles for

Early settlers often came into the valley with their families and all their belongings piled onto one wagon. The wagon in this 1889 photo was pulled by a four-horse team. The photograph was taken near Ramon Road and South Palm Canyon Drive.

PALM SPRINGS DESERT MUSEUM COLLECTION

Dr. Welwood Murray, a native of Edinburgh, Scotland, came to the United States at the age of 26 to work as copyreader for a publishing firm. Records show Murray arrived in the tiny settlement of Banning, California in 1876 where he became manager of the San Gorgonio Fluming Company. He later purchased eighty acres in Banning and began ranching and raising fruit. These crops marked the beginning of Banning's flourishing orchards. Murray acquired the title "Dr." during the Civil War when he tended the wounded on a warship. Murray soon became an important resident of Palm Springs. The cemetery which bears his name, in which he, his wife and young son are buried, was donated to the Palm Springs Cemetery District in 1917 by his family. The Welwood Murray Library, at the corner of Palm Canyon Drive and Tahquitz Canyon Way, was a gift to the city from his heirs. Murray Canyon and Murray Hill are also named after him.

PALM SPRINGS HISTORICAL SOCIETY COLLECTION

sale. During his first eight years, he bought more than six thousand acres of land, primarily from the Southern Pacific Railroad. In 1887, three hundred twenty acres were surveyed into a township, recorded in October 1887, that today comprises downtown Palm Springs. That year an auction was held and one hundred thirty-seven parcels were sold for a total of more than $50,000.

In 1887 McCallum and three other men founded the Palm Valley Land and Water Company, which was incorporated with 5,000 shares at $100 per share. Nineteen miles of rock-lined cement ditches were built to bring water to Palm City from Snow Creek, Whitewater River and Chino and Tahquitz canyons.

Farmers who bought acreage from McCallum soon began planting a variety of crops to determine which ones would flourish in the irrigated desert. Alfalfa, grapes, corn, figs, apricots, grapefruit and oranges were harvested, and experiments were conducted with date palms.

With an increasing population came the need for a general store. McCallum refurbished an old building and stocked it with staples for settlers, feed for livestock and necessities for desert travelers. He named it Palm Valley Store.

Although he wanted to sell more land, there was no place for prospective buyers to stay when they arrived to look over the area. He convinced Dr. Welwood Murray, a leading citizen from Banning, to build a hotel on five acres across from the hot springs. Murray then leased the hot springs from the Indians and built a bath house for the patrons. The Palm Springs Hotel became Palm City's first resort-oriented business.

The question of water rights arose when developer B. B. Barney purchased six hundred acres from McCallum and Van Slyke, who also gave them the water rights. Barney built a subdivision called The Garden of Eden, at the present-day site of the Canyon Country Club. Streets were named for Adam, Eve and other biblical characters. Barney piped in water from Andreas Canyon, which was actually owned by the Indians, and started a series of litigations that lasted for many years. (Because he was the Indian Agent, McCallum had given Barney the water rights. This transaction was later found to be illegal by the courts. As part of the settlement with the Agua Calientes, the U. S. Government bought the interests of the owners of the Garden of Eden, which by then was deserted.)

John McCallum contracted for nineteen miles of rock-lined irrigation ditches to bring precious water to Palm Springs from Whitewater and Snow Creek. The flume was completed in 1887.

PALM SPRINGS DESERT MUSEUM COLLECTION

Land sales were booming in 1888 in Palm Valley, generally known as Palm Springs after 1887. Special trains transported prospective buyers from Los Angeles and San Francisco to the Seven Palms station across the valley. After disembarking, passengers were driven in carriages and buckboards across six miles of desert wasteland to Dr. Murray's hotel paradise.

Everything flourished until about 1890. Impressive fruit orchards dotted the landscape, and alfalfa and row crops thrived. Unfortunately, the abundance was short-lived. An all-time record rainfall was recorded in 1893. The torrential downpour lasted twenty-one days and washed out miles and miles of irrigation ditches. Other ditches filled with sand, cutting off the farmers' lifeline.

The first farmers in Palm Springs experimented with many crops, including date palms. The newly planted shoots from mature trees required careful irrigation in the arid climate.

PALM SPRINGS DESERT MUSEUM COLLECTION

Promoter B.B. Barney called his subdivision The Garden of Eden when the development was laid out in Sections 35 and 36 at the present intersection of Murray Canyon Drive and South Palm Canyon Drive. Circular streets surrounding a site for the proposed Grand Hotel Eden were named after biblical males: Adam, Ophir, Abraham, Noah and Nimrod. The spoke streets were called Eve, Miriam, Sarah, Mary, Ruth, Naomi, Rachel, Timma, Hannah and Leah. Water for the project was delivered via a flume from Andreas Canyon, depriving the Indians at Rincon of their water. After years of litigation, the Federal government bought out the settlers and gave Section 35 to the Indians. It is the only odd-numbered section now owned by the Indians, who often spoke of the "serpent in the Garden of Eden" – meaning developer Barney. For years, while legal skirmishes slowly took their course, the only resident on the property was Adam Weed, a fitting name for the abandoned project's caretaker.

PALM SPRINGS HISTORICAL SOCIETY COLLECTION

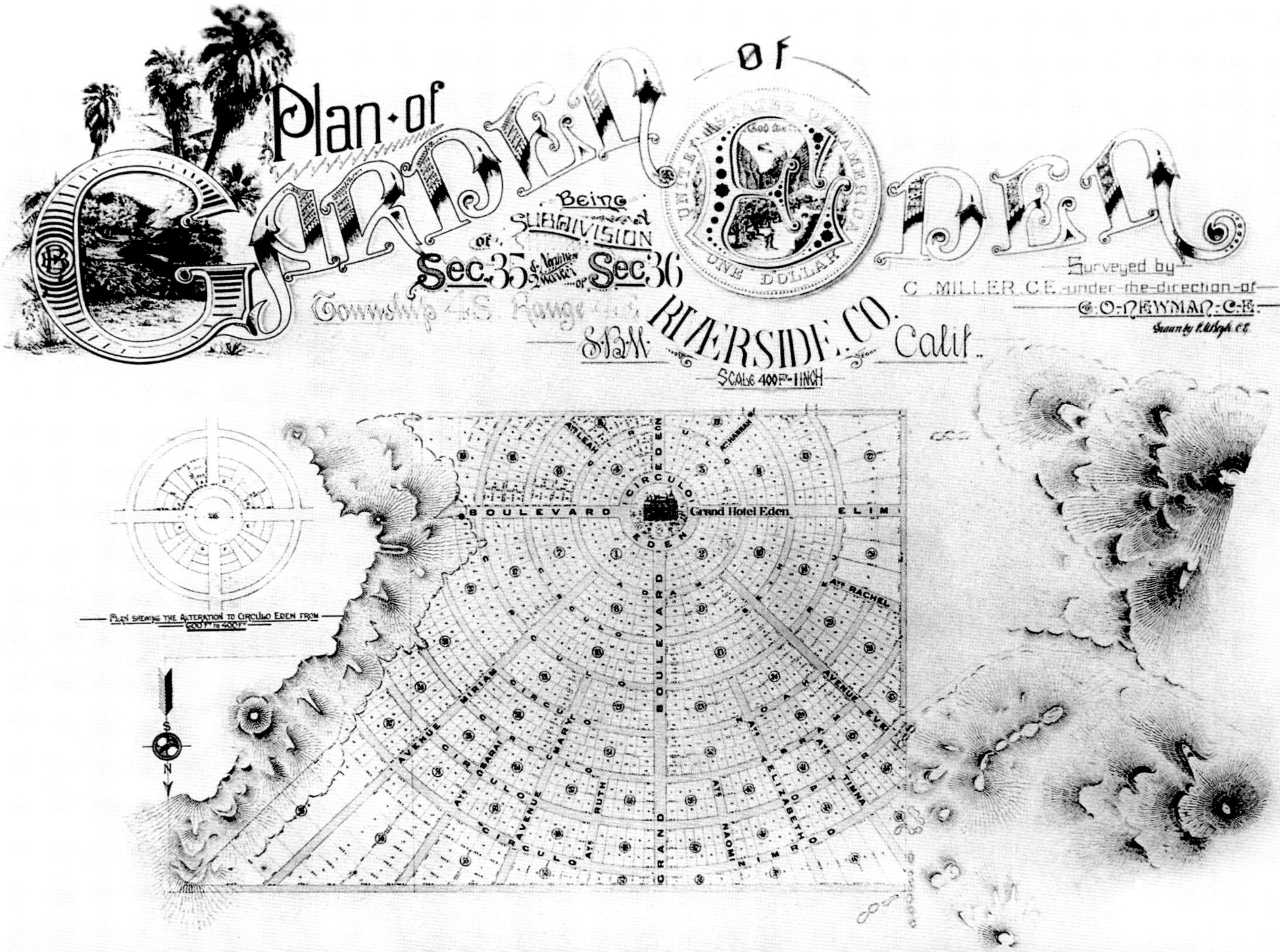

Plan of Garden of Eden
Being a Subdivision of Sec. 35 Sec. 36
Riverside Co. Calif.
Surveyed by C. Miller C.E. under the direction of G.O. Newman C.E.
Scale 400 ft = 1 inch
Boulevard
Grand Hotel Eden
Circulo Eden
Grand Boulevard

It was not until January 15, 1916, that a paved highway opened connecting the growing village of Palm Springs with Banning. It was the first desert county highway permanently improved in the state of California. Seated at the table with members of the Riverside County Highway Commission is Nellie Coffman *(far right)*, owner of The Desert Inn where the opening ceremony was held. A model of the road is shown in the center of the table. Standing along the side at the left are members of the Agua Caliente Band of Cahuilla Indians with Dr. Harry Coffman *(foreground, far left.)*

PALM SPRINGS HISTORICAL SOCIETY COLLECTION

The devastation didn't end there. After the crop damage was repaired and irrigation ditches cleaned out, an eleven-year-long drought hit the region, drying up the ditches and forcing settlers to drink the highly sulfuric water from the mineral springs.

McCallum's dream of a desert oasis ended when most of the settlers moved away from the area. Devastated by his son Wallace's death in 1896 and deeply in debt, he died in 1897 believing his life a failure. His estate included almost six thousand acres of land, stock in the water company, and some farm equipment and livestock.

By the time the drought ended in 1905, it was too late for farmers to save their crops; most of the grapevines and fig trees were dead. Settlers were trying desperately to sell their land. As payment for a small bank claim, the widow McCallum surrendered her controlling shares in the Palm Valley Water Company. They were acquired by Ralph Rogers, a land developer, who proceeded to clear out the nineteen miles of irrigation ditches and restore water to the village.

Emily McCallum died in 1914. Their daughter Pearl inherited the remaining land. Through her strong will and determination, she built upon her inheritance and left a legacy that is discernible in the Coachella Valley to this day.

ABOVE: The road from Palm Springs to the town of Banning traveled around Windy Point, often passing through deep sand. The route sometimes took three hours when the wagon was heavily loaded. The photograph is of Pearl McCallum driving her three-horse team on the route in 1904.

PALM SPRINGS DESERT MUSEUM COLLECTION

RIGHT: Campers in 1896 at Indian Wells, one of the important watering stops on the old Bradshaw Trail, a route taken by Californians seeking gold in Arizona Territory. It is believed that Chief Cabezon supplied stage driver Bill Bradshaw with directions for the route to the gold discoveries on the Colorado River. The trail began in Redlands, California, stopped at desert watering holes such as the Indian village at Palm Springs; Indian Wells; Dos Palmas; Brown's Pass; Chuckwalla Wells; Ehrenberg, Arizona; and ended finally in La Paz in the Territory of New Mexico, now Arizona.

FRANK BOGERT COLLECTION

ABOVE: Land sales were booming in California in 1887 when a subdivision called Palmdale was begun near the present site of Smoke Tree Ranch. A narrow gauge railroad was built from Seven Palms mainline station across the valley in a direct line for the Palmdale site. After considerable difficulty, the railroad was completed. Passenger service began with a small wood-burning locomotive named "Cabazon," three flat cars for baggage and freight, and two San Francisco cable cars still displaying their bay area destination signs "Market Street" and "Sutter Street." After only a few months of operation, the railroad ran out of money, and the locomotive and cars sat forlornly on the desert until 1892, when the last engineer, A.D. Spring, hauled the engine, two flat cars, and most of the rails to Bakersfield. Two cable cars remained on the desert until they were burned about 1910 by surveyors in the area. Several houses were built from the ties, including Miss Cornelia White's home, now relocated in the Village Green Heritage Center on South Palm Canyon Drive.

PHOTO BY J. SMEATON CHASE, PALM SPRINGS HISTORICAL SOCIETY COLLECTION

RIGHT: The McCallum mountain home and orchards (in the area of the present Tennis Club, at the west end of Baristo Road), were on eighty acres in Section 15. McCallum harvested alfalfa fields and grew a wide variety of fruit and melons on his fertile land. He sold his crops, including grapes, figs, apricots and oranges, in Los Angeles where a good price was obtained because of the desert's early growing season. This photograph, taken in 1894 at the beginning of the disastrous eleven-year drought, shows McCallum's ranch already drying up. Records show that most of the early residents soon became discouraged and left the area with only a few families remaining in the village, among them the McCallums, Murrays, and the Indians. Only twenty non-Indian adults were counted as residents as the drought continued.

PALM SPRINGS HISTORICAL SOCIETY COLLECTION

BELOW: An unidentified young family photographed by A.B. Trott in 1898 were among the early home builders living on McCallum's subdivision in Section 15 of Palm Springs.

PALM SPRINGS HISTORICAL SOCIETY COLLECTION

Before drought destroyed most of McCallum's orchards, the ditch carrying water from nearby canyons flowed full amid his lush orange groves. The water wheel filled water storage barrels.

PALM SPRINGS HISTORICAL SOCIETY COLLECTION

RIGHT: In the summer of 1905, John Muir showed up unexpectedly at Welwood Murray's hotel with his two daughters, Wanda and Helen.
PALM SPRINGS HISTORICAL SOCIETY COLLECTION

LEFT: A lazy afternoon of croquet for guests at Dr. Murray's Palm Springs Hotel. It was in 1887, at the insistence of his friend John McCallum, that Murray decided to purchase ten acres of land in Palm Springs, twenty-four miles away from where he then lived in Banning. Murray, quickly recognizing the new community's potential, constructed a hotel in the center of town. He continued his experiments with citrus, exotic fruit trees, and shrubs on the adjacent acreage, becoming a leading horticulturist in California. During summer months, Murray lived in Banning, soon becoming a leading citizen of both communities.

PALM SPRINGS HISTORICAL SOCIETY COLLECTION

BELOW: Elizabeth Erskine Murray, wife of Dr. Murray, was born in Scotland in 1830. While her husband worked on horticultural experiments, she taught at the Potrero Reservation Indian School in Banning. After the Palm Springs Hotel was built, Mrs. Murray took charge, becoming well-known for her nursing abilities and good, home-cooked meals. Before long, the hotel boasted of entertaining guests from all over the world. Many wrote glowing letters about her motherly care, the pleasant accommodations, Indian baths and dry desert climate that quickly cured their ailments.

PALM SPRINGS HISTORICAL SOCIETY COLLECTION

ABOVE: A Southern Pacific Railroad section house was located across the mainline tracks from the railroad station at Whitewater. The photographer was an eastern civil engineer, Frank Elwood Brown, who was in the area surveying and checking drainage conditions around Mt. San Jacinto and Mt. San Gorgonio in 1898.

PALM SPRINGS DESERT MUSEUM COLLECTION

EXCURSION
—TO—
PALM SPRINGS,

LEAVES LOS ANGELES ON S. P. R. R.,

October 31st, at 8 A. M.

Rate of Fare for Round Trip.

San Francisco to Seven Palms, and return $25 00
Los Angeles, San Gabriel, Monte and Pomona, and return 3 50
Ontario and Cucamonga, and return :............... 3 40
Colton, and return 2 70

Take train leaving S. P. R. R. depot at Los Angeles at 8, a. m. Monday, October 31st, reaching Seven Palms at 12:20, p.m. Leaves Colton at 10:20 a. m. Returning on any regular train in two or three days.

Invest at Palm Springs, where there is

NO FROST!
NO HEAVY WINDS!
NO FOG!

THE HOME
OF THE
BANANA, DATE AND ORANGE.

Only Spot in California where Frost, Fog and Windstorms are Absolutely Unknown.

The Earliest Season in the State. Best Opportunity for Men of Moderate Means. Every Fruit and Vegetable Matures a Month to Six Week's Earlier than Anywhere Else on the Coast.

RIGHT: Advertisement promoting travel to Palm Springs, as printed in the *San Bernardino Weekly Times* of October 29, 1887.

PALM SPRINGS HISTORICAL SOCIETY COLLECTION

LEFT: A winter visitor from Dr. Murray's hotel explores the pools in upper Palm Canyon.

PALM SPRINGS HISTORICAL SOCIETY COLLECTION

Hotel guest A.B. Trott photographed proprietor Welwood Murray and lady guests at a picnic in Palm Canyon about 1898. Trott's notes on the back of the photo identified the home towns and the tourists enjoying themselves in the California desert resort: Miss Gussie Koch and Miss Locke, Los Angeles; Mrs. Culver of Port Townsend, Washington; Mrs. Koch, Los Angeles; Mrs. Walker, Louisville, Kentucky; Misses H. and R. Ulrich, Springfield, Illinois; and Miss Boyd, Riverside.

PALM SPRINGS HISTORICAL SOCIETY COLLECTION

RIGHT: Off to the Indian canyons for a picnic, guests of Welwood Murray's hotel travel by mule-drawn buckboards with a bearded Murray in the last wagon.

PHOTO BY A.B. TROTT, PALM SPRINGS HISTORICAL SOCIETY COLLECTION

ABOVE: During the Spanish-American War in 1898, guests of the Palm Springs Hotel decided to show the colors and demonstrate their patriotism with the rifles on hand. FROM LEFT TO RIGHT: Frank McQuoid, San Francisco; Andrew West, Los Angeles; an unidentified local Indian; L. Wagoner, San Jose; A.B. Trott and A.F. Jones, Brooklyn, New York; G.F. Casey, St Louis, Missouri; Col. William Roy, Nogales.

PALM SPRINGS HISTORICAL SOCIETY COLLECTION

RIGHT: Guests of the first hotel in Palm Springs pose for photographer A.B. Trott, about 1898. Mrs. Walker, from Louisville, Kentucky, at center in white hat, was a yearly hotel guest.

PALM SPRINGS HISTORICAL SOCIETY COLLECTION

In 1898, a favorite way to while away relaxing hours at the Palm Springs Hotel was a game of bridge and a few beers. Notice the empty beer bottles hanging from the trunk of the date palm.

PALM SPRINGS HISTORICAL SOCIETY COLLECTION

Photographer A.B. Trott of Brooklyn, New York, poses at an Indian well in 1898, now the location of the city of Indian Wells. This well replaced the deep Cahuilla well that had been there for centuries.

PALM SPRINGS HISTORICAL SOCIETY COLLECTION

BELOW RIGHT: Photographer Trott's hotel bill for a month's stay in Palm Springs in 1898: Room and board – $35; films and developing – $2.30.

PALM SPRINGS HISTORICAL SOCIETY COLLECTION

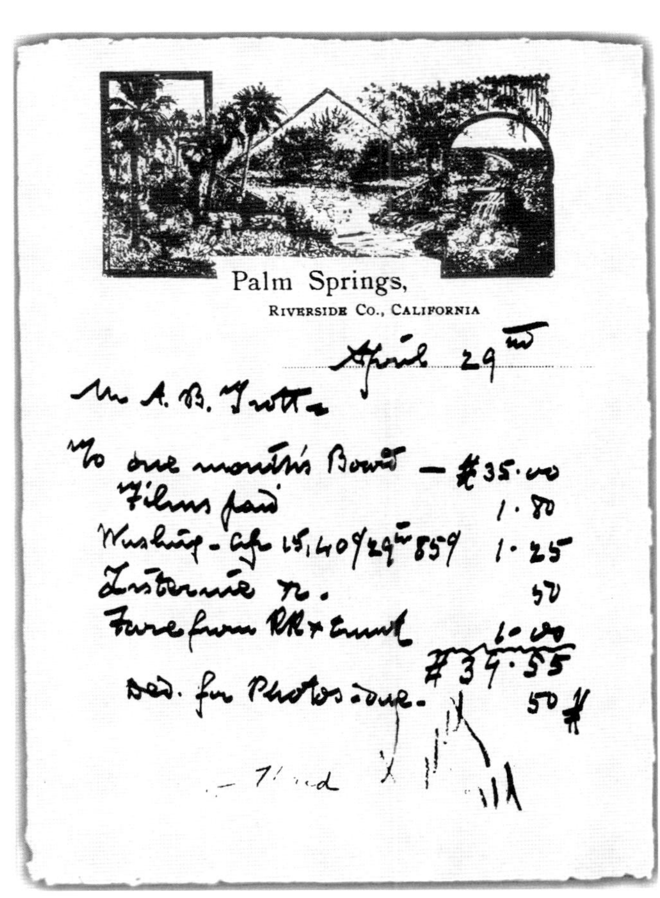

Palm Springs,

RIVERSIDE CO., CALIFORNIA

April 29th

Mr A. B. Trott

To one month's Board —	$35.00
Films paid	1.80
Washing - Apr 15, 40/29th 859	1.25
Listerine [illegible]	.50
Fare from RR & trunk	1.00
	$39.55
Ded. for Photos due.	50

LEFT: The most outstanding natural feature of Palm Springs is the hot spring in the center of town. Indians may have inhabited the region for five hundred to one thousand years. In 1887 Dr. Welwood Murray built the first hotel, located as close as possible to the hot spring, which he had leased from the Indians for $100 a year. The bathhouse and dressing rooms were erected directly over the spring. The original bathhouse remained on the site until 1916, when the Indians razed the structure and built their own bathhouse. The rickety bathhouse had two rooms, the larger covering a pool big enough to allow four people to stand together in the hot curative waters. It was impossible to sink because of the silt-like mud covering the bottom. Indian and white children playing in the spring would often dare one another to sink to the bottom. The children would let go of the protective railing surrounding the spring and try to push a playmate under the water only to have the child quickly pop back up to the surface. Lena Lugo Martinez recalls how after a bath the children would run outside the bathhouse without any clothes to play in the cool, sulphur-smelling water in the shade of nearby palms.

PALM SPRINGS HISTORICAL SOCIETY COLLECTION

Downtown Palm Springs in 1900, looking southeast.

PALM SPRINGS HISTORICAL SOCIETY COLLECTION

The warm, dry climate of Palm Springs attracted many people seeking a cure for tuberculosis, although hotel managers seldom mentioned the illness. Lavinia Crocker opened one of the first sanatoriums in 1898. The facility was later purchased in 1910 by Dr. Harry and Nellie Coffman.

PALM SPRINGS HISTORICAL SOCIETY COLLECTION

An early prospector with his pack burros rides out of Palm Springs across the desert. *[Eds. Note: This photograph was actually taken c. 1945 by a Hollywood makeup artist who costumed his wife to look like a prospector.]*

PALM SPRINGS HISTORICAL SOCIETY COLLECTION

HOTEL.
STORE.
OFFIC

LEFT: Homes of Palm Springs' first white settlers about 1920 in what is now downtown Palm Springs. To the northeast are the snow-capped Indio Hills and Little San Bernardino Mountains.

PALM SPRINGS HISTORICAL SOCIETY COLLECTION

Agua Caliente Indians Rosa and Marcus Belardo were a popular couple with village settlers. Marcus is at the wheel with wife Rosie by his side and passengers Dr. Harry Coffman, *right*, and Mr. Winters, a tuberculosis patient at The Desert Inn Sanatorium, c. 1913.

PALM SPRINGS HISTORICAL SOCIETY COLLECTION

LEFT: Ralph Rogers on the porch of an early hotel run by David Blanchard about 1910, when classical architectural motifs were not part of the marketing program for the embryonic resort.

PALM SPRINGS HISTORICAL SOCIETY COLLECTION

ICE-CREAM
YOGURT
PANTRY
HEATRE

3

Creating a World-Famed Resort

Though greatly disheartened by losing so many of his experimental trees during the drought, Dr. Welwood Murray doggedly hung onto his hotel. In 1908, he attempted to sell the property to Nellie Coffman and her son Earl during their visit to the hotel. Although Murray was unsuccessful, Nellie returned with her husband, Dr. Harry Coffman, and two sons the following year. They bought Lavinia Crocker's Sanatorium a block away and across the street from Murray's hotel.

After purchasing Mrs. Eleanor Martin's house, which adjoined the property on the north, they added a few more tent houses and opened Dr. Harry Coffman's Desert Inn and Sanatorium. For several years the Inn catered solely to people suffering from asthma, arthritis and similar ailments. Their brochure made no mention of "tuberculosis;" Nellie's guests miraculously acquired "bronchitis" as soon as they registered.

Around 1915, Dr. Harry and Nellie Coffman decided that Palm Springs should become more than just a haven for people who were ill. When her husband moved to Calexico about 1917 to start a medical practice, Nellie and her sons, George Roberson and Earl Coffman, started their hotel. Their new brochure specified "no invalids," thereby excluding anyone with a communicable disease.

Mother Coffman, as she was affectionately called by the villagers, and her sons kept adding to their property. They had paid a premium to buy out Lavinia Crocker, then secured a bank loan and added new bungalows and a new dining room. By 1926, following the construction of new, mission-style buildings, The Desert Inn had become a world-renowned hotel.

Nellie practically ran the town by virtue of her strong will and personality. If a patron saint were chosen for the valley, it should be this extraordinary lady pioneer.

LEFT: The luster of Palm Springs never dims. Classic cars line up on Palm Canyon Drive just south of Tahquitz Canyon Way. Gleaming in the background is the Plaza Theater, the desert's oldest theater, home to the "Fabulous Palm Springs Follies."

PHOTO BY KIRK OWENS

PREVIOUS PAGES: A cattle drive by the Talmadge brothers in the summer of 1914 from the desert to Big Bear Valley, a ride often joined by sisters Cornelia and Florilla White. Frank and Will Talmadge ran cattle in the Coachella Valley and in the high desert as far as Twentynine Palms.

PALM SPRINGS HISTORICAL SOCIETY COLLECTION

Nellie Coffman arrived in Palm Springs in 1908. An intelligent, honest and determined woman, she helped to shape the future of the Coachella Valley.
PALM SPRINGS HISTORICAL SOCIETY COLLECTION

Dr. Murray, a great contributor to early progress, died in 1914. The White sisters, Florilla and Cornelia, bought his hotel and the rest of the block to the south and nearly all of the land in what is now the 100 block north and 100 block south of Palm Canyon Drive. They quickly became a driving force in the village, a role they would hold for many years.

Pearl McCallum McManus returned to Palm Springs to find herself virtually unknown. Because Nellie Coffman's reputation was so wide-spread, considerable rivalry developed between the two women. Pearl's obvious move was to build a hotel. She and husband Austin amassed enough money to hire a young architect, Lloyd Wright, son of Frank Lloyd Wright, to design a hotel.

Their Oasis Hotel opened in 1925 on land Judge McCallum had settled in 1885. Later, when the McManuses added twenty-six rooms to the hotel, a new location had to be found for McCallum's original adobe house. Eventually, in 1953, Pearl and Austin employed local architect William F. Cody to dismantle the building and move it brick by brick to the Village Green on South Palm Canyon Drive, where it stands today.

A lack of money kept the McManuses from furnishing the hotel. W. E. Hanner, who had previously owned the Cecil Hotel in Los Angeles, took over the hotel operations. Several small hotels also made their debuts: Otto Adler's La Palma Hotel, a block north of The Desert Inn; the Tauchers' Winter Garden; and the Goff family's hotel. John and Frank Miller's family bought the Monte Vista Apartments, converting them into a hotel which still stands.

Artists, writers and photographers, most of whom had come to the desert for their health, soon spread word of its beauty and beneficial climate. Among the first of the world-famous visitors was John Muir, already well-known from his books and the discovery of the Alaskan glacier that bears his name. Muir was also the founder of the Sierra Club and instrumental in establishing Yosemite National Park. With daughters Wanda and Helen, he traveled to the desert because of Helen's illness. They arrived unexpectedly at Welwood Murray's hotel in the summer of 1905 when the temperature was already in the 110° to 120° range and the hotel was closed for the season. After a few days' stay in the unbearable heat, the trio moved to Andreas Canyon for the remainder of their two-week visit. There, Muir was joined by T.P. Lukens of the U.S. Forest Service.

Another well-known writer, naturalist and photographer was J. Smeaton Chase, who married the third White sister, Isabel. His book, *California Desert Trails*, published in 1919, was widely read as was his smaller volume, *Our Araby,* the story of Palm Springs. All of his works were illustrated with his photographs, several of which are included in this book.

The Wonders of the Colorado Desert, by George Wharton James, was published in 1907. It contained more than three hundred sketches by artist Carl Eytel, who also wrote articles for the *Los Angeles Times* and a German newspaper. Hundreds of his pen and ink sketches and paintings did much to publicize Palm Springs.

W.W. Lockwood, who came to Dr. Coffman's sanatorium afflicted with tuberculosis in 1911, was the first professional photographer to visit the area. For several years he took hundreds of excellent photographs of the region.

Stephen Willard, who arrived in 1917, was acclaimed as a scenic photographer. His photos and beautiful hand-painted enlargements were sold throughout the country and are still preserved as classic works in many museums.

One of the The Desert Inn's first guests was Jimmy Swinnerton, a nationally known cartoonist sent to the desert for his health by newspaper magnate William Randolph Hearst. He spent many winters in the desert resort and was described as a one-man chamber of commerce for Palm Springs.

Edmund Jaeger, one of the village's first school teachers, became renowned as a botanist and desert authority. His articles and books on the desert gained wide recognition.

Local residents join visitors at a camp in Andreas Canyon about 1912. Jimmy Swinnerton is standing at the far left; Edmund Jaeger and Welwood Murray are on the right.

PALM SPRINGS HISTORICAL SOCIETY COLLECTION

The Clatworthy family, early residents of Palm Springs, lived in a home on the north side of Ramon Road. Fred Clatworthy was a world-famous color photographer, whose photographs were often featured in *National Geographic.* Shown here at Tahquitz Ditch, are the women of the Clatworthy family in a typical magazine pose: daughter Helen pours cool water into her canteen while sister Barbara looks on; supervising is their mother Mabel.

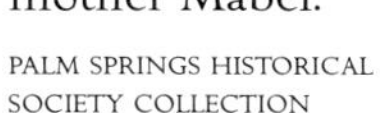
PALM SPRINGS HISTORICAL SOCIETY COLLECTION

Fred Payne Clatworthy, a long-time village resident, was a pioneer in color photography. His photos, which first appeared in *National Geographic* in 1923, were among the first color photographs published by that magazine.

By this time, many other photographers and travel writers had discovered Nellie Coffman's Desert Inn. The *Los Angeles Times* regularly carried illustrated stories, and Jimmy Swinnerton made sure that the Hearst papers gave the village wide publicity.

Anthropologists discovered that the elder members of the Indian band were a wealth of information on Cahuilla culture. Lucille Hooper published her book on the Cahuilla Indians in 1920, following it with several papers on the tribe that were published by the University of California around 1925.

Edward Curtis had photographed the local Indians in their canyon homes even earlier than 1920. William Strong's book, *Aboriginal Society in Southern California,* devoted much space to the Cahuillas, as did A.L. Kroeber's book, *The Handbook of the Indians of California.* Both books were published in 1925.

Life in the village was slow and easy during this period. It consisted of checking at The Desert Inn for any new and interesting guests, stopping at Carl Lykken's store and post office for mail or to take a look at any new merchandise, walking down the street to say hello to other residents or to see how Lois Kellogg's house was progressing, or listening to the local gossip at Dr. Kocher's drugstore.

The village by this time boasted a library, grammar school and a volunteer fire department. Among the downtown businesses were a barber shop and a few curio shops, including Fred Watson's Indianoya.

At night you had dinner at La Palma Cafe, where beautiful Jennie Leonesio was a waitress, or played a game of pool and ate a plate of spaghetti at Harry Mutascio's restaurant. Twice a week you could go to the grammar school and watch a movie shown by Earle Strebe.

An occasional party at The Desert Inn or in a private home was attended by everyone in town, including the local cowboys, hotel guests and shopkeepers.

Never afraid of hard work or getting her hands dirty, part-time resident and true eccentric Lois Kellogg digs a ditch to help with construction of Fool's Folly, as she called her home, which was never finished.
PALM SPRINGS HISTORICAL SOCIETY COLLECTION

Horseback riding was the most popular outdoor recreation. Both Harriet Cody and Charley Wise had livery stables from which groups headed for rides into the canyons. Most of the village children had Indian ponies, which they rode bareback all around town. Shaded by large cottonwoods, Indian Avenue made a good straightaway for the occasional horse race.

Charley Wise was an old-time cowboy with a harelip who was as colorful as a Damon Runyan character. Other interesting townspeople included Zaddie Bunker, a mechanic in the Bunker Garage, who drove a truck long before most women were doing such things, and Frankie Paul, a half-Mexican wrought-iron worker, whose iron gates and silver-inlaid bits and spurs are still around.

The biggest event of the season was the annual Indian pageant, the *Desert Play,* started in 1921 by Garnet Holm and held each year at the entrance

Beautiful Harriet Cody came to Palm Springs for her husband's health. Harold Cody, a successful Hollywood architect, had moved to the dry desert to cure his recurring bouts of pneumonia. Harriet took care of her husband, raised their daughter Patsy and started the first livery stable in town. When Harold died in 1924 she bought eighty acres that she subdivided and started the first rental stable with over thirty-five horses. In later years she ran a small hotel on South Cahuilla Road called Casa Cody.
PALM SPRINGS HISTORICAL SOCIETY COLLECTION

One of the biggest tourist attractions in the 1920s was the *Desert Play* held at the mouth of Tahquitz Canyon. Local citizens were actors. Here are Pat Cody, daughter of Harriet Cody, and Theil McKinney, in full costume for the 1921 spectacular.

PALM SPRINGS HISTORICAL SOCIETY COLLECTION

to Tahquitz Canyon. Many Indians and a number of other residents were enlisted as actors. Tickets for the event, usually staged the first week in November, cost one dollar and attracted large crowds from Los Angeles and surrounding towns. Mary Austin wrote the first spectacular, entitled *Fire*. The next year's production, *Tahquitz the Evil One*, was based on local Indian mythology.

By 1918, the town was large enough to warrant a local government to handle such matters as roads, sanitation and promotion. A Board of Trade was formed with Dr. J.J. Kocher as president. Board members included Carl Lykken, Cornelia White, George Roberson, Oliver McKinney, P.T. Stevens, Ed Bunker and others.

It was 1928 before a Fire Protection District was formed. Alvah Hicks, Carl Lykken and George Roberson served on the supervisory committee. Sanitation was handled by Caesar Spalleti, a Swiss-Italian who lived on the Indian reservation. He would stand in front of the post office to collect his monthly fees for garbage pickup.

For many years, Joe Toutain was the local constable under the Police Protection District and Willie Pablo was the Indian law.

The town's first telephone was in Carl Lykken's store. Southwest Home Telephone brought in their first service in 1927; by the end of the year they had over one hundred subscribers. Electricity was furnished by Southern Sierra Power Company, which had over two hundred connections by 1927.

During the 1920s, Palm Canyon and other palm-lined Indian canyons received considerable publicity when a huge effort was made to make them part of a national monument. In *Our Araby*, J. Smeaton Chase wrote that the canyons were a national park. He jumped the gun, however, as the Indians refused to accept the ridiculously low offer of $22,000 for 1,600 acres.

In the winter of 1924, over 35,000 tourists visited the canyons. Hermit's Bench, the natural strip of land above Palm Canyon where the parking lot and trading post are located, was crowded every weekend of the season. Most of the tourists came only to view this spectacular area, returning to their homes the same day.

To many of today's residents, it is surprising how few people stayed in the village during the summer. By the middle of each June, primarily Indians, business owners, their employees and their families remained. Many people, such as Nellie Coffman, had summer homes in Banning or Idyllwild. Harry Mutascio's cafe was the first business to have air-conditioning. It would be another thirty years before Palm Springs became a year-round resort.

Harry Mutascio *(below)* stands in front of his pool hall and lunch counter before it became a full-fledged restaurant. Harry arrived in Palm Springs in 1922 from Genoa, Italy, via New York. Working as a stone mason with his brother-in-law, John Barone, he saved enough to buy six pool tables in Los Angeles for five dollars each. After repairing them, he built a pool hall across the street from the La Palma Hotel. Five cents was the charge to play a game of pool or watch a movie. His wife Josephine's *(above)* good cooking soon prompted him to add a restaurant, which he successfully ran until 1945. He sold it to Irwin "Ruby" Rubenstein, who operated the establishment as Ruby's Dunes. Today the building has a new front but is still located in the 200 block of North Palm Canyon Drive where it has housed a succession of restaurants and bars.

PHOTO COURTESY BARBARA MUTASCIO

Prescott T. Stevens, a successful cattle rancher from Colorado, arrived at The Desert Inn around 1912. During the next ten years Stevens purchased most of the land in the north end of town from the Southern Pacific Railroad, built a home and became one of the most active citizens in Palm Springs. He helped Alvah Hicks develop Vista Acres subdivision and later sold much of the land that is today the Las Palmas area. He bought several shares in the Palm Valley Land and Water Company and formed the Whitewater Mutual Water Company to distribute the irrigation water for the village. In 1926, Stevens formed a company to build the El Mirador Hotel, *(right)* which opened one year before the 1929 stock market crash. The hotel failed and the $750,000 project was sold to the bondholders for $65,000 in 1932, saddling Stevens with a heavy burden of debt. He died shortly afterward, leaving the water company to his daughter, Sallie, and her husband, Culver Nichols.

PALM SPRINGS HISTORICAL SOCIETY COLLECTION

Colorado cattleman Prescott T. Stevens, an early Desert Inn guest, built a house in the village, acquired a considerable amount of land in the north end of the city and helped create the Whitewater Mutual Water Company. In 1926, he organized a company to build the El Mirador Hotel, financing the project with $750,000 in bonds, most of which were held by Ralph Lacoe from San Diego.

The hotel opened in 1928, but in the wake of the stock market crash of 1929 and the subsequent Depression, by 1932, the year that Stevens died, it was having serious financial problems. It was the worst disaster suffered by the village during these years. Though Alvah Hicks had a few foreclosures in his Las Palmas subdivision and a small number of houses were taken over by banks, the village was not affected as seriously as other cities.

Los Angeles attorney Warren Pinney was hired by the El Mirador investors to protect their interests. Pinney and Lacoe acquired the hotel for $65,000 and reorganized with Pinney as manager and Lacoe as majority owner.

Pinney created a glamorous resort with bellboys in fancy uniforms: Gus, the doorman, greeted guests in a general's uniform; Tom Cooney, the chef, was noted for his fine cuisine and lavish buffets; and Dovey Cooley, hostess, saw that guests never lacked an amenity. The hotel garage, usually filled with Rolls Royces and Cadillacs, was equipped with eight chauffeurs' rooms. The Desert Inn met the challenge of this competition. Most of the guests were a sedate group who preferred the Old World charm and hospitality offered by Nellie Coffman. Shirley Temple and several other movie stars were loyal to the Inn, but most of the Hollywood group patronized the El Mirador. Both hotels catered primarily to Eastern and Northwestern tourists who came by train with large steamer trunks and stayed for a month or all season.

Around this time, Charlie Doyle started two dude ranches. Deep Well Ranch, a property that local banker Phil Boyd later purchased in bankruptcy, was operated as a hotel by Boyd and partners Frank and Melba Bennett. Smoke Tree Ranch was the site of an 1887 land development called Palmdale. Fred Markham bought the property and, with the help of Raymond Cree, subdivided it into the present Smoke Tree Colony. The original dude ranch

The El Mirador Hotel was built by Prescott T. Stevens and opened in 1928. It became the hotel of choice for the Hollywood crowd. Today the site of Desert Regional Medical Center, only a replica of the bell tower remains.
PALM SPRINGS HISTORICAL SOCIETY COLLECTION

is still operated as a successful hotel and exclusive residential community.

In the early days, Hollywood studios were used only for close-up scenes; Palm Springs served as a location site for Arabia, North Africa, Mexico and other international areas. As many as ten movies were made each season and both guests and townsfolk turned out to watch the proceedings.

Fatty Arbuckle, Theda Bara, Ernest Torrence, Louise Lovely, Dustin Farnum and Rudolph Valentino were but a few of the stars who became part of the social scene. Local gossips reported that Valentino rode over to see Lois Kellogg whenever he came to Palm Springs to work on a picture.

By 1936, Ralph Bellamy and Charlie Farrell's Racquet Club had attracted even more of the Hollywood set. The Club had no visitor accommodations for many years, so people stayed in hotels and guest ranches all over the village. Later, Charlie bought out Ralph's interest, and he and his wife Virginia Valli operated the Club. Their membership consisted of the Hollywood elite and a large number of the local gentry. It was a haven for starlets hoping to be noticed by one of the of many movie moguls sunning around the pool. Many contracts were consummated at the Club.

The Chamber of Commerce replaced the Board of Trade. Most of the civic leaders from

Dr. Albert Einstein was a world-renowned scientist in 1933 when manager Warren Pinney invited him to stay at the El Mirador as his guest. His appearance guaranteed the hotel international publicity. Ernst Lubitsch, famous Hollywood producer, appears to be asking Einstein the name of his tailor. *Left to right:* Pinney's daughter Phyllis, Warren Pinney, Mrs. Einstein, Dr. Albert Einstein, Ernst Lubitsch and Louella Pinney, Warren's wife.

PALM SPRINGS HISTORICAL SOCIETY COLLECTION

the earlier days remained on the board of directors: Carl Lykken, George Roberson, Harold Hicks, Earl Coffman and Earle Strebe. Added were Warren Pinney, Frank Bennett and Francis Crocker. Though the chamber handled publicity and advertising, the two large hotels also had public relations staffs.

Samuel Untermyer, a Desert Inn guest, later built a house on property to the south. The first attorney in the country to receive over a $1 million fee, he was the village's first nationally known millionaire. At his invitation, Dr. and Mrs. Albert Einstein visited Palm Springs. Tony Burke's photos of the couple covered the globe. After their stay with the Untermyers, Warren Pinney invited them to extend their visit at the El Mirador.

Untermyer's next guest was the flamboyant Jimmy Walker, mayor of New York. As he was under investigation at the time, his presence brought reporters from both wire services and national newspapers to the village. Earl Coffman arranged a fake holdup of the train, and the good mayor was transported to the village in a stagecoach followed by a group of local riders and cowboys.

Other prominent guests included Auguste and Jean Piccard, famous Swiss scientists who had set records in balloon ascents and submarine descents, and General Atterbury, president of the Pennsylvania Railroad. John Jacob Rascob, owner of the Empire State

Building, an annual visitor to the El Mirador, bought twenty-five hundred acres of land in Desert Hot Springs.

By 1936, hotels in the booming village were showing an eighty percent occupancy rate. Charles Chamberlin and Alvah Hicks were building many new houses in the exclusive Las Palmas district, and Robert Ransom talked Mrs. Julia Carnell, owner of the National Cash Register Company of Dayton, Ohio, into buying Miss Cornelia White's three and one-half acres. The result was La Plaza, later owned by Stanley Rosin and Zachary Pitts.

Desmond's, Maloof's and several smaller shops also opened in 1936. Two prestigious department stores opened: Bullock's on the grounds of The Desert Inn and I. Magnin at the El Mirador Hotel.

Palm Springs was in the beginning of its heyday, with many first-class hotels, excellent shopping, and a world-wide reputation as "America's Foremost Desert Resort." Movie stars such as William Powell, Cary Grant, Bob Hope, Frank Sinatra, Phil Harris and a host of others built homes; Darryl Zanuck, Joe Schenck and many other movie moguls made the village their winter home. A list of the residents of the Las Palmas and Deep Well communities read like *Who's Who in American Business.*

The quaint little village was about ready to become a city.

Desert Gold, a Famous Players-Lasky movie was shot on location in the desert about 1925 and starred William Powell.

COURTESY MRS. WILLIAM "MOUSIE" POWELL, PALM SPRINGS HISTORICAL SOCIETY COLLECTION

Photographer Stephen Willard *(left)* is shown below on a photo excursion in his 1920 Chalmers. The finest scenic photographer of his time, Willard captured deserts, canyons and mountains in a classic collection of black and white photographs *(right, top)* and hand-tinted photographs and postcards *(right, bottom)*. He was a meticulous photographer; his photographs were noted for their fine composition and choice of subject matter. The Willard family home still stands today on the grounds of Moorten Botanical Gardens.

PHOTO COURTESY BETTIE WILLARD,
PALM SPRINGS HISTORICAL SOCIETY COLLECTION

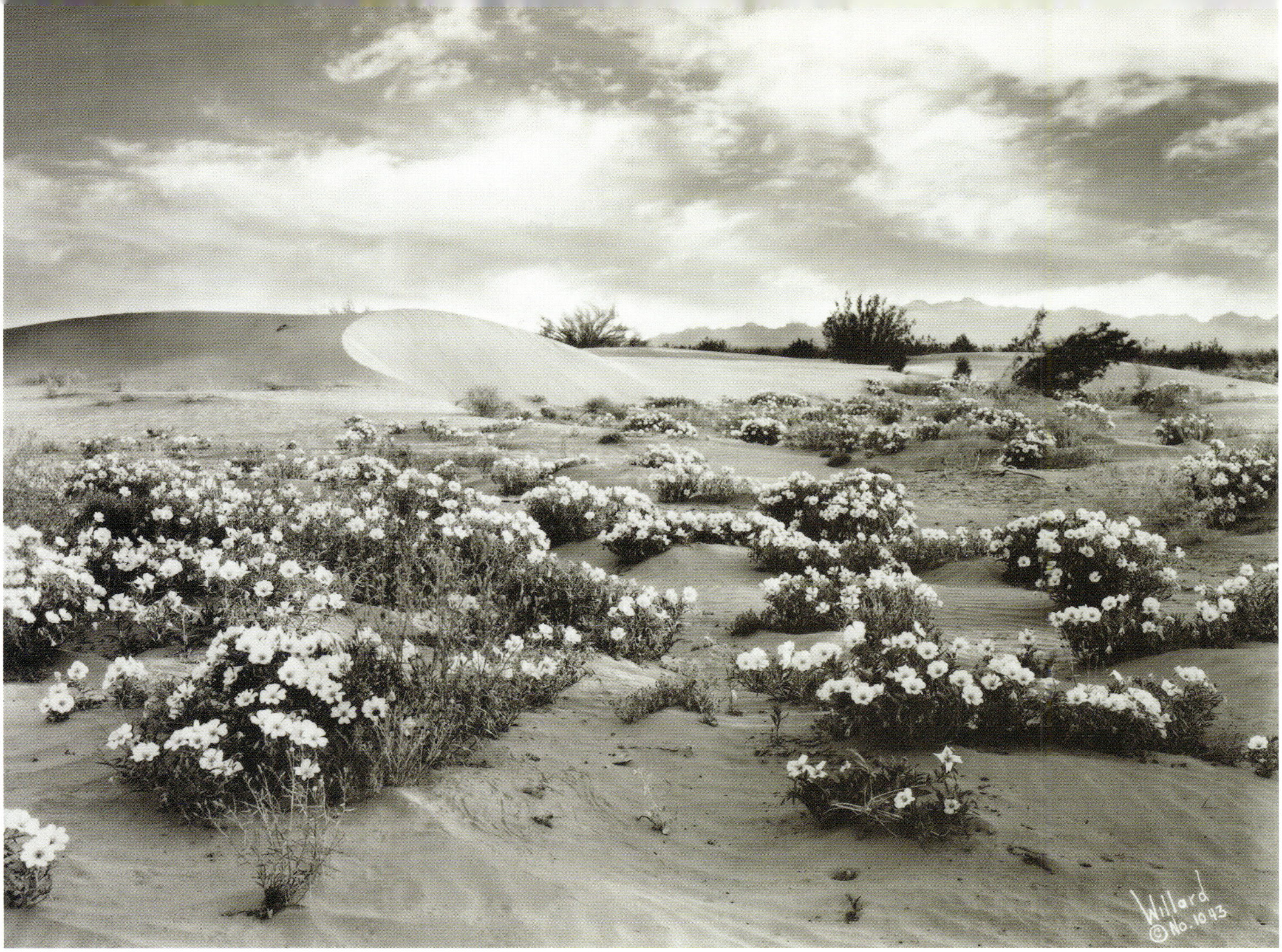
Willard
© No. 1043

Willard ©
A-11

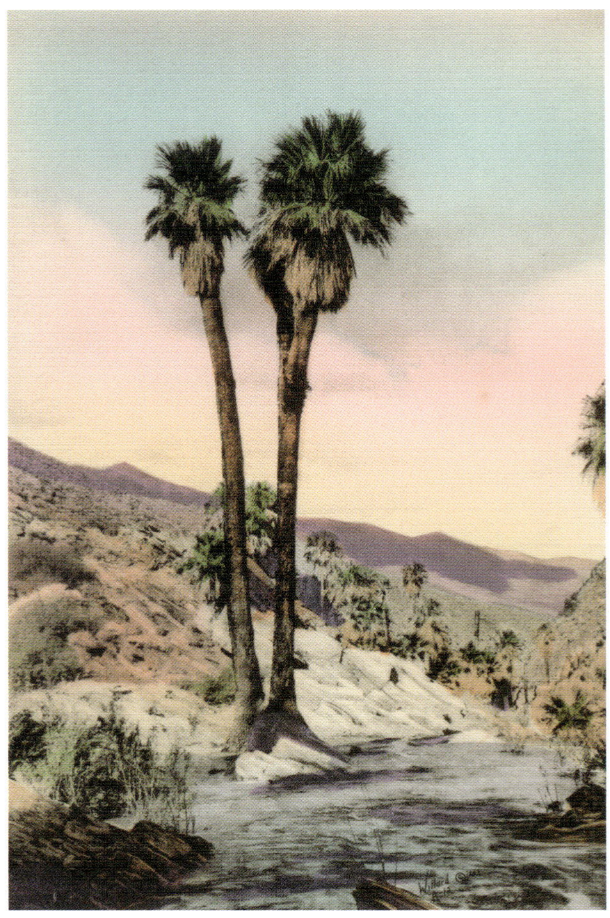

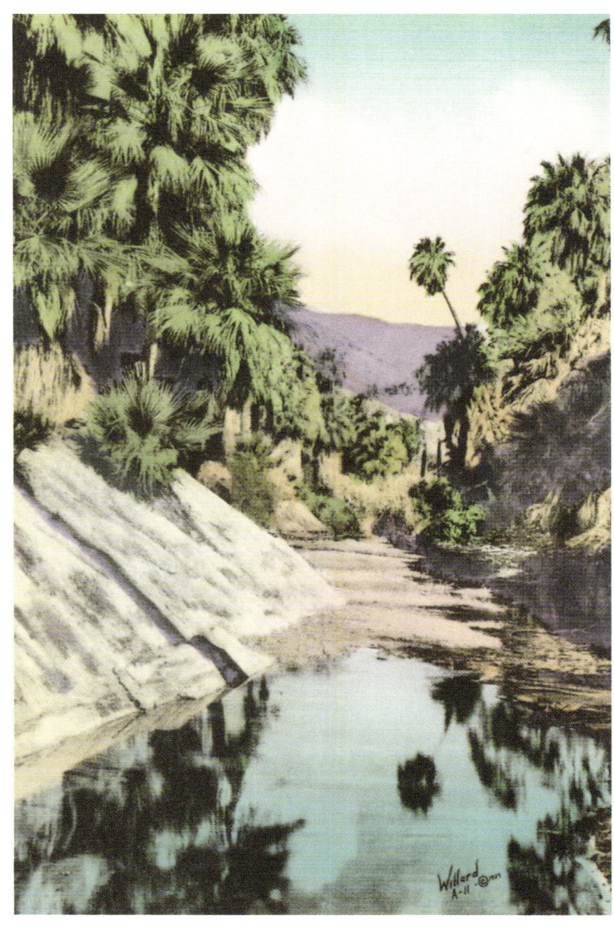

Pearl McCallum McManus

The story of Pearl McCallum McManus, written by Katherine Ainsworth in her book, *The McCallum Saga,* reads like imaginative fiction. Pearl arrived in Palm Springs with her family in 1885 at the age of 6. An amazing woman, McManus blossomed during the last thirty years of her life. When she died on July 24, 1966, at the age of 87, she left a legacy that contained hundreds of contributions to the city. She and her husband Austin built the Oasis Hotel and the Hacienda Apartments and developed the city's first major subdivision, Tahquitz River Estates, which contained Robinson's department store, the Tennis Club and many individual homes. Austin was a careful businessman, who managed the properties and made it possible for Pearl to keep her acreage from which she derived a substantial income.

Over the years she donated a fortune to a number of charities, colleges and museums. After her death, the McCallum Foundation gave millions of dollars to colleges and city projects, including the airport fountain, the Village Green where the Palm Springs Historical Society is located, McCallum Desert Park on El Cielo with the equestrian center (now Tahquitz Creek Golf Resort) and the McCallum Theater in Palm Desert.

McManus did not want her name identified with these projects, insisting on honoring her father, John Guthrie McCallum. Through her efforts, the McCallum name is on streets, buildings, parks and colleges and is almost a byword of the valley. Judge McCallum would be very proud of the daughter who picked up the pieces following the desert drought and put everything back together. She contributed greatly to the economic growth of Palm Springs in addition to donating millions of dollars to the desert community.

Pearl McCallum shares a chair with her brother Wallace in the yard of their family's Los Angeles home.

PALM SPRINGS HISTORICAL SOCIETY COLLECTION

LEFT: Pearl McCallum McManus at 79 still enjoyed outings with the Desert Riders. At the stable she always requested "a good lively horse."

PHOTO BY FRANK BOGERT

A 1956 family reunion at the home of Mrs. Pearl McCallum McManus celebrating the birthday of Mrs. Walter McManus, Pearl's sister-in-law. *Seated:* Harold Rounds III, Robin Petri and Gerald Rounds; *Middle row:* Pearl McManus, Sally McManus holding baby Michael, Mrs. Harold Rounds, Mrs. Talma Tanner (sister of Austin McManus) and Mrs. Vernon Petri. *Top row:* Joan McManus, David McManus, Harold Rounds and Vernon Petri.

PHOTO BY VIC CULINA, SALLY McMANUS COLLECTION

One year before she died in 1966, Pearl McManus cut the cake celebrating the thirty-fifth anniversary of the Desert Riders. *From the left:* President M. A. "Boo" Hoff, Melba Bennett from Deep Well Ranch, Pearl and Tony Burke.

PALM SPRINGS HISTORICAL SOCIETY COLLECTION

David Manley Blanchard

Like many of the early pioneers, Blanchard came to the desert in 1889 to cure his consumption. He started a small store, ran the post office, was the local barber and offered rentals in a four-room hotel and several tent houses. His store, between what are now Indian Canyon Drive and Palm Canyon Drive on Andreas Road, was the only source of supplies after McCallum closed his small shop. He sold groceries, some hardware and ice, which he hauled each week from the railroad station.

After he sold his business to Carl Lykken and J.H. Bartlett in 1915, he moved to Banning, completely cured of tuberculosis. Blanchard died at age 69 from a fall.

In the late 1800s, David M. Blanchard ran a small general store that was later purchased by Carl Lykken and J.H. Bartlett. Blanchard managed the first post office and also rented several tent houses to people suffering from tuberculosis.

PALM SPRINGS HISTORICAL SOCIETY COLLECTION

Carl Eytel

Although Palm Springs and environs are a favorite subject of many artists, Carl Eytel was the first to sketch and to paint the desert as it actually looked. Born in 1862 in Stuttgart, Germany, Eytel came to the United States in 1885. He arrived in Los Angeles in 1898 and a few months later discovered the small desert village of Palm Springs. The McCallum family gave Eytel permission to build a cabin beside their irrigation ditch, a site near the present Tennis Club.

Carl roamed the entire Coachella Valley from the Salton Sea to Banning, making accurate sketches of historic buildings (all of which are gone today). His pen and ink drawings, particularly of palms, have never been equaled by another desert artist. He sold his works to anyone who would pay prices that were barely enough to cover his expenses for art supplies and meals. In 1906, George Wharton James hired Carl to do over three hundred drawings for his book, *Wonders of the Colorado Desert.*

Carl became a close friend of fellow-artist Jimmy Swinnerton; the pair often took off on sketching trips into the desert. He was also a friend of many local Indians, learning their language, customs and ceremonial songs.

Carl Eytel died in a Banning sanatorium in September 1925, at the age of 63, from chronic tuberculosis and was buried in the Indian cemetery in Palm Springs after a ceremony at The Desert Inn ramada. Eytel is one of the few white men ever accorded this honor by his good friends, the Agua Caliente Indians.

The Palm Springs Desert Museum, Palm Springs Historical Society and the Southwest Museum in Los Angeles preserve his sketches, paintings and writings in their collections. In 1979, the Palm Springs Desert Museum published *Forgotten Desert Artist,* a book by Roy Hudson that contained much of Eytel's life's work.

Carl Eytel painting his much-loved palms in Palm Canyon.

PALM SPRINGS DESERT MUSEUM COLLECTION

A group of tourists heads for Indian Wells on a five-hour trip by mule team. Carl Eytel (at the reins) copied this photo for a sketch now in the archives of Southwest Museum in Los Angeles.

FRANK BOGERT COLLECTION

Carl Eytel sits in the doorway of his house on McCallum land. The house was built from lumber salvaged from settlers' homes abandoned during the drought of 1894.

PALM SPRINGS HISTORICAL SOCIETY COLLECTION

LEFT: Palms on the old switchback trail in Palm Canyon are depicted in a typical Carl Eytel pen and ink sketch. Palms were artist Eytel's favorite subject; he loved to sit near them under varying conditions of sun and shadow, sketching the slender stems, green frond fans and modest dry skirts of the ancient palms. Even in his lifetime, Eytel was known as "The Artist of the Palm."

SKETCH COURTESY OF SOUTHWEST MUSEUM

W.W. Lockwood, Palm Springs' first professional photographer.

PALM SPRINGS HISTORICAL SOCIETY COLLECTION

Jimmy Swinnerton worked in New York in 1906 as one of newspaper publisher William Randolph Hearst's foremost cartoonists. After he contracted tuberculosis, Hearst sent him, a doctor, and a nurse to Colton, California. By 1907 he had recovered sufficiently to take a trip to Palm Springs, where he met Carl Eytel. The following year he moved to Dr. Coffman's sanatorium and later into a tent home known as The Sidewinder Shebang. Thanks to Nellie Coffman's good food and the beneficial climate, Jimmy recovered completely. For nearly seventy years, the Swinnertons were either arriving or departing Palm Springs. His fame as a cartoonist was forgotten as he received national acclaim as a landscape and desert painter, with one-man shows in major cities across the country. When he died in Palm Springs in 1974, he was ninety-nine years old. At age 31 he had been sent to California with only one year to live.

PALM SPRINGS HISTORICAL SOCIETY COLLECTION

The A.E. Davis family home is typical of a 1912 Palm Springs residence. Built from canvas and wood, it was similar in construction to the tent houses at The Desert Inn.

PHOTO BY W.W. LOCKWOOD, PALM SPRINGS HISTORICAL SOCIETY COLLECTION

ABOVE: By the mid 1930's, The Desert Inn occupied 35 acres in downtown Palm Springs. Facilities included a swimming pool, tennis courts, golf course and horseback riding. Services included a house physician and a brokerage office.

PALM SPRINGS HISTORICAL SOCIETY COLLECTION

LEFT: The main entrance to The Desert Inn was on what are now Palm Canyon Drive and Tahquitz Canyon Way. It later became the offices of Doctors Hill and Oliver. This photo taken by W.W. Lockwood in 1911 shows only Dr. Coffman's plaque hanging at the front.

PHOTO COURTESY JOHN MILLER

Before World War I, The Desert Inn's guests were picked up at the Southern Pacific railroad station six miles north of Indian Avenue by the Inn's stage operated by George Roberson. Photo shows Earl Coffman and guest in the stage. Dr. Harry Coffman is driving the buckboard.

PALM SPRINGS HISTORICAL SOCIETY COLLECTION

Desert Inn guests relax in front of one of Nellie's tent houses in 1912.

PALM SPRINGS HISTORICAL SOCIETY COLLECTION

LEFT: A proud Marcus Belardo shows his date palm to The Desert Inn owner Dr. Harry Coffman in 1912. Dates were considered an exotic luxury by guests. The biblical association of dates and The Desert Inn's asserted "curative value" were stressed by management.

PALM SPRINGS DESERT MUSEUM COLLECTION

BELOW: Little Virginia McKenzie and her mother, Mrs. Bernard McKenzie, on the porch of their Palm Springs home about 1906. The home was later sold to Nellie Coffman. Virginia became Mrs. W. Murray Smith of San Diego.

PHOTO COURTESY MRS. W. MURRAY SMITH

Residents of Palm Springs celebrated Nellie Coffman's eightieth birthday on November 1, 1947 with an 1890's party. With her are her two sons George Roberson *(left)* and Earl Coffman.

PHOTO COURTESY GEORGE VALEUR

ABOVE: Earl Coffman, H. Earl Hoover and Dr. William Colburn look on as Miss Cornelia White presents the deed for the Palm Springs Desert Museum property on March 28, 1947. From the day of Miss Cornelia White's arrival in Palm Springs, she never wore skirts. Her daily uniform for forty-five years was riding pants, leather puttees, safari jacket and African pith helmet. She was seen everywhere in the valley in this costume, exploring the desert on horseback for forty miles in every direction, and joining the Talmadge brothers on their annual cattle drive from the desert to Big Bear Valley.

PALM SPRINGS HISTORICAL SOCIETY COLLECTION

LEFT: Dr. Florilla White of Utica, New York, who dressed like her sister, Cornelia, arrived in the village in 1912. Miss Cornelia, who had been living in Nayarit, Mexico, followed shortly thereafter. The White sisters purchased the old Palm Springs Hotel property from Welwood Murray, as well as the block immediately south of the hotel. They continued to rent rooms, without meals, handling most of the overflow from The Desert Inn. Dr. White, an ardent horsewoman, was active with the Desert Riders and spent days in the mountains with Lee Arenas exploring the canyons and streams.

PALM SPRINGS DESERT MUSEUM COLLECTION

A possible route for a big race promoting the Coachella Valley/San Gorgonio road to Los Angeles is being studied. Earl Coffman is at the wheel, with George Roberson beside him; an unidentified woman is perched on the hood. The license plate reads, "Loaned by the National Motor Car Company."

PALM SPRINGS HISTORICAL SOCIETY COLLECTION

In 1912, the Banning Route Boosters were promoting the road through the Coachella Valley and San Gorgonio Pass as the best route to Los Angeles from the east. On this National Highway Tour, twenty-two carloads of passengers stopped overnight at The Desert Inn on the road from Yuma and the Imperial Valley to Los Angeles.

PHOTO BY W.W. LOCKWOOD,
PALM SPRINGS HISTORICAL SOCIETY COLLECTION

The first paving of Main Street, now Palm Canyon Drive. Yeager Construction Company of Riverside received the paving contract about 1915. In the background is The Desert Inn.

PALM SPRINGS HISTORICAL SOCIETY COLLECTION

While the main street in Palm Springs was paved after 1915, side roads leading into the desert were not. Cars stuck in the sand were a common problem. Sometimes a four-horse team was needed to extract the errant vehicles, even those equipped with chains on their rear wheels.

PALM SPRINGS HISTORICAL SOCIETY COLLECTION

Alvah Hicks

Alvah Hicks came to the desert in 1913 to homestead a plot four miles north of Seven Palms. (The homestead was near what is now Pierson Boulevard and Indian Avenue, just north of Garnet.) Hicks was a carpenter, and, until 1917, he commuted to Los Angeles to work, even though there was considerable construction taking place in Palm Springs. Assisted by P.T. Stevens, he acquired twenty acres in the village, subdivided it, and built several houses, all of which he sold quickly.

Hicks organized the Palm Springs Water Company and the Palm Springs Builder's Supply. By the 1930s, he and his wife Tess, as she was known to the villagers, became prominent civic leaders. Alvah assisted with the city's incorporation and served on the first city council.

He was an excellent horseman and one of the founders of the Desert Riders and the Polo Club. Until his death in 1945, he was a member of every important board in town. Tess died two years earlier. After his death, son Harold took over the reins at the water company and son Milt managed the Builder's Supply.

At their homestead near North Palm Springs, Alvah and Theresa Hicks pose with their sons, Milton, *left* and Harold.

PHOTO COURTESY HAROLD HICKS

RIGHT: Pioneer Alvah Hicks building Lois Kellogg's mysterious home called Fool's Folly.

PALM SPRINGS HISTORICAL SOCIETY COLLECTION

Carl and Edith Lykken in their popular Palm Springs Department and Hardware Store. The building remains and has housed a number of businesses. Carl Lykken was one of Palm Springs' outstanding pioneers.

PALM SPRINGS HISTORICAL SOCIETY COLLECTION

Carl Lykken

Carl Lykken was one of Palm Springs' foremost pioneers. Arriving in 1913 after helping to found an American colony in Nayarit, Mexico, Lykken and a partner, J.H. Bartlett, purchased a small store in the village. Later, Lykken erected a wooden building on Main Street (now in the 100 block of North Palm Canyon Drive). His store soon became a combination post office, dry goods, grocery and hardware store. He ran the telegraph for Western Union having purchased the town's first telephone from Welwood Murray. The line ran out to the train station at Garnet.

Lykken served the city of Palm Springs for fifty-nine years, until his death at age 87. He was a founding member of the Police Protection District, Fire Department, Sanitary Commission, Rotary Club, Community Church, Polo Club, Desert Riders and Desert Museum, and served as president of the Palm Springs Chamber of Commerce. Lykken and his wife Edith were perhaps the city's most beloved citizens. Their daughter Jane Hoff was reared in Palm Springs. Following in her father's footsteps as a community leader, she became an active member of the Palm Springs Historical Society Board of Directors.

Carl Lykken and his assistant Clarence Templeton in front of his general merchandise store, which boasted the only telephone in town.

PALM SPRINGS HISTORICAL SOCIETY COLLECTION

Lois Kellogg

Lois Kellogg, originally from Chicago, was the wealthy and beautiful daughter of Ambassador Pierpont Ishan Kellogg. She arrived at The Desert Inn in 1914 for just a visit, but soon became enamored of the desert. She met Harriet Cody, Zaddie Bunker and the White sisters, making friends in a short time. Soon the former socialite and world-traveler was exploring the country on horseback, and, on one occasion actually captured a wild mustang on a trip into Palm Canyon, a horse she kept until she died.

In 1921, Kellogg started construction on her Moroccan-style home, hiring Harriet Cody's husband, Harold, as architect and Alvah Hicks as carpenter. Lois, her friends, and local Indians worked on the elaborate house that she named Fool's Folly. Many photographs were taken during the building, showing Lois working on the house, digging ditches and putting shingles on the roof. When Harold Cody died in 1924, work stopped. The home was never completed. Lois lived in a few finished rooms with her Russian wolfhounds, and kept the wild mustang and four Charolais bulls in an adjacent corral, before moving them to Norman Farra's stable.

After many years in Palm Springs, Lois finally moved to Tonopah, Nevada, to raise Russian wolfhounds. She died there in 1943. Her uncompleted home remained abandoned for many years, with only occasional occupancy by adventurous local children. Irwin Schuman eventually bought the property for use as a Jewish temple classroom. He later built the first Safeway market there, located on the east side of South Palm Canyon Drive in the 300 block.

Lois Kellogg was a former Chicago socialite who took a liking to the wide open spaces of early Palm Springs.

PALM SPRINGS HISTORICAL SOCIETY COLLECTION

Analysis of water in the Indian hot springs as described in Otto Adler's Hotel La Palma brochure

(milligrams per liter):

METABORIC ACID (BO_2)	TRACE
SILICA (SIO_2)	44.8
SULPHURIC ACID (SO_4)	37.3
CARBONIC ACID (CO_3)	33.0
BICARBONIC ACID (HCO_3)	36.6
NITRIC ACID (NO_3)	0.1
CHLORIN (CL)	25.0
IRON (FE)	1.9
CALCIUM (CA)	2.5
MAGNESIUM (MG)	0.7
SODIUM (NA)	67.5
	249.4

PALM SPRINGS DESERT MUSEUM COLLECTION

The first bathhouse, *above*, was built in the 1870's. By 1914 the Indians had razed and rebuilt it, *below*. The property, still operated by the Tribe, is now the site of the Spa Resort and Casino.

PALM SPRINGS HISTORICAL SOCIETY COLLECTION

Dr. Edmund Jaeger gained wide acclaim as a prominent desert authority. Probably no other man in the area was more involved with the preservation of natural resources. Many of his books were important references for students of desert and mountain flora and fauna. Jaeger's books were also popular with visitors seeking less technical information about the wonders of Southern California. Though he spent most of his later years in the Riverside area, Palm Springs is proud to have had him as an adopted son for a short time, a time which he regarded as "among the happiest days of my life."

PALM SPRINGS HISTORICAL SOCIETY COLLECTION

Dr. Edmund Jaeger, who taught school in Palm Springs in 1915, gained fame as a botanist and world-renowned desert authority. Students in the front row: Ellen Maxwell, Franklin Smith, Stella Block, Frances Bunker, Jackie Robinson and Perry Brown. In the top row: Annie Pierce, Kermit Maxwell, Jaeger, and Justin and Douglas Smith.

PALM SPRINGS HISTORICAL SOCIETY COLLECTION

Photographer J. Smeaton Chase was not only a prolific photographer but a well-known author. He arrived in Palm Springs in 1915 and married Miss Isabel White, one of the three White sisters, three years later. Born in London in 1864, he died in Banning in 1923. He wrote a number of books on California, including *Our Araby: Palm Springs and the Garden of the Sun* and *California Desert Trails.*

PALM SPRINGS HISTORICAL SOCIETY COLLECTION

Carl Diebold, also known as Dutch Frank, was a familiar sight in the early 1900s around Palm Springs. He was short, had a thick German accent, and spent much of his time searching for gold from Banning to the Salton Sea and from Twentynine Palms to Idyllwild. Writers visiting the area during these years wrote glowing tales of their adventures and explorations with Dutch Frank.

PALM SPRINGS HISTORICAL SOCIETY COLLECTION

A 1914 photo of Zaddie, Frances and Ed Bunker near Chino Canyon on their way to a new home in Palm Springs.

PALM SPRINGS HISTORICAL SOCIETY COLLECTION

In the 1920s, Zaddie Bunker managed Bunker's Garage. Later, in the 1940s, the building became the popular Village Pharmacy on North Palm Canyon Drive and Andreas Road. The site later became an upscale shopping mall.

PALM SPRINGS HISTORICAL SOCIETY COLLECTION

Zaddie Bunker

Zaddie and Ed Bunker were among the very few healthy people who came to Palm Springs in the early days. They arrived in town in 1917 in their heavily-laden, two-cylinder Maxwell car. For two years they lived in a tent while Ed worked as a blacksmith in his shop on the corner of Andreas Road and Palm Canyon Drive. The shop later became Bunker's Garage. Eventually they bought all the property they could personally manage and built the Bunker Cottages.

Ed Bunker, whose first name was Chauncey (hardly an appropriate name for a blacksmith and cowboy), left the village to run the Bunker Ranch in Garner Valley. Zaddie, who was quite a proficient mechanic, stayed to run the garage. When George Roberson went overseas during World War I, she took over his passenger stage service with an old truck that she had reassembled. She drove the daily stage to meet the Southern Pacific train to pick up passengers and freight destined for Palm Springs during the war and kept the old Moreland truck in good shape until Roberson returned in 1920. Zaddie became one of the first women in California to receive a chauffeur's license.

Over the years, Zaddie sold or leased her property on Palm Canyon Drive and bought land in many parts of town as she could afford it. After her daughter Frances married Earle Strebe, Zaddie and Earle worked together on many projects. They built the Palm Springs Theater, known locally as the Village Theater. They leased a portion of the 200 block on North Palm Canyon Drive to Jack Freeman for his Freeman's Desert Grill. The restaurant was later sold to Irwin Schuman for his Chi Chi nightclub and restaurant.

At 65, Zaddie earned her pilot's license and bought her own plane, entered the Powder Puff Derby, and won fame across the country as the "flying grandmother." The U.S. Air Force invited her to Edwards Air Force Base where she flew in a jet and became one of the first women to fly faster than the speed of sound.

Even after Zaddie was quite wealthy, she could be seen every morning sweeping the walks in front of the Village Pharmacy and the theater. When the Desert Fashion Plaza was built in 1984, Zaddie's grandchildren received over $5 million dollars for the property where the Bunker Garage and the Village Theater had stood for so many years.

Frances Bunker, daughter of Zaddie, drives her personal burro cart around the village. Frances, who later married Earle Strebe, had three daughters: Geska, Dorothy and Susan.

PALM SPRINGS HISTORICAL SOCIETY COLLECTION

During World War I, while George Roberson was in military service, Zaddie Bunker took over his job driving the daily stage to bring guests and supplies to the village. Zaddie was one of the first women in California to acquire a chauffeur's license.

PALM SPRINGS HISTORICAL SOCIETY COLLECTION

Oliver and Rose McKinney celebrate their fiftieth wedding anniversary. The McKinneys arrived in Palm Springs in 1917 with five children, a chicken coop, two tents, and a dutch oven for cooking. Digging one well for Raymond Cree led to digging another, and owning a tripod hoist led to planting palms and giant saguaros on local estates and hotel grounds. The business evolved into The Desert Nursery, owned and operated by the family for twenty years from 1925 to 1945.

PALM SPRINGS HISTORICAL SOCIETY COLLECTION

The McKinney Family

Superintendent of Schools Raymond Cree hired Oliver S. McKinney to dig a water well on his date ranch in 1917. At the time, the McKinney family lived on their homestead in Morongo Valley. McKinney went to work for Cree, and with his wife and five children, moved to Palm Springs where after digging several wells and planting palms, he started a business called The Desert Nursery. In 1924, the McKinneys purchased ten acres in the 600 block of South Palm Canyon Drive for $240 in back taxes. He built twenty small rental units and a trailer park as a place for working people to stay. Eventually McKinney acquired an eighty-acre farm in the Deep Well area at Camino Parocela, Sunny Dunes and South Palm Canyon Drive.

Rose and Oliver were the parents of eight children: Eldon, Willard, Glen, Arol, Theil, Ted, Don and Barbara. Their son Ted was thought to be the first non-Indian child born in the village. He was on the Palm Springs City Council for twelve years, on the Indian Planning Commission and the board of the Palm Springs Historical Society. Glen owned a local blacksmith shop; Arol became an accomplished horsewoman and managed a stable; Theil returned to Morongo Valley where she ran a beauty salon; and the youngest daughter, Barbara, operated the very successful Desert Car Wash for many years.

Eighty-five years later, there have been five generations of McKinneys. It is difficult to remember a time when at least one McKinney wasn't in the Palm Springs school system.

One of the more interesting characters living in the area around Palm Springs in 1917 was young William Pester. He had a cabin in Palm Canyon and another next to a hot spring in Chino Canyon, where he lived during the summer months. He was the first "nature boy," putting on clothes, often a monk's robe, when curious canyon visitors came into view. He earned a living making canes from palm blossom stalks, fashioning Indian arrowheads and selling postcards with a message urging proper diet and healthful living. Though he spent many hours roaming the canyons, he had an equal passion for reading. Years later a large library was discovered in his deserted cabin. In the 1920s, Pester moved from Palm Canyon but returned every weekend with his telescope, charging ten cents to look at the moon or at Lincoln's profile on Mt. San Jacinto, *left*. The profile can still be best seen today from the corner of Palm Canyon Drive and Amado Road, though few people notice it. The reproduction at left is from a postcard sold by Pester.

PALM SPRINGS DESERT MUSEUM COLLECTION

The "angel" on the mountain was another Palm Springs natural feature that every visitor viewed. Though much darker and overgrown with bushes, it is still visible. Angel View Crippled Children's Foundation is named for this natural attraction.

FRANK BOGERT COLLECTION

The road into Palm Springs was a one-lane oiled surface in 1921. Passing was done carefully as the sand on each side was very soft. Windy Point is at the end of the road; the rock formation on the left is at the mouth of Chino Canyon.

PHOTO BY HUMPHREY BIRGE, FRANK BOGERT COLLECTION

Palm Springs Presbyterian Church

Organized March 27th 1917 with nineteen Charter Members coming from five Different Denominations. Rev. J. P. Mac Phie Minister in Charge at the time.

Names of Charter Members:

Rev. Thomas D. Christie D.D.,
M. S. Gordon
Chauncey E. Bunker sr.
Mrs. Cynthia A. Bunker
Mrs. Ann M. Pennington
Mrs. Lavinia F. Crocker
Edith E. Call
Orion Hatchitt
Mrs. Alice Kirkpatrick
Joseph A. Setter
Mrs. Elizabeth C. Mac Phie
Mary Isabel Mac Phie
Meda Stein
Mrs. Zaddie Bunker
Carl G. Lykken
Florence Kirkpatrick
Dr. J. J. Kocher
Mrs. J. J. Kocher
Josiah Gentry

First Christmas services at the old Palm Springs Presbyterian Church. Located at the corner of Palm Canyon Drive and Andreas Road, the church was used until 1935. It was organized on March 27, 1917, with nineteen charter members from five different denominations. The lot was later sold for $40,000 to build the new Palm Springs Community Church on Baristo Road.

PALM SPRINGS HISTORICAL SOCIETY COLLECTION

The first Easter Sunrise Service was held on Sunrise Point April 8th 1917.

Shown here are charter members of the first Palm Springs Presbyterian Church, established in 1917. In 1986, a group of Palm Springs residents once again formed a branch of the church.

PALM SPRINGS HISTORICAL SOCIETY COLLECTION

Dr. John Jacob Kocher was a practicing physician and pharmacist. He opened his own drugstore opposite The Desert Inn main entrance on Palm Canyon Drive, calling it the Mortar and Pestle. The mortar rock at the entrance was donated by Oliver McKinney. On November 21, 1917, when Dr. Kocher opened for business, most of the first customers signed the guest book. It is interesting to note the mixture of local residents, hotel guests and tribal members which made up society during this period.

PALM SPRINGS HISTORICAL SOCIETY COLLECTION

Dr. and Mrs. Kocher were feted at a "stork party" of young pioneers in 1936 to celebrate babies he had delivered. *Bottom row:* Bobby Bell, Nick Mutascio, Helen Louise Williams holding Dr. Kocher's hand and Dr. Kocher. *Top row:* Mrs. Kocher, Ted McKinney, Carmela Mutascio, Barbara McKinney, Bettie Willard, Elizabeth Coffman, Owen Coffman, Vyola Hatchitt and Frankie Bellue. Many of those children are still residents of Palm Springs.

PALM SPRINGS HISTORICAL SOCIETY COLLECTION

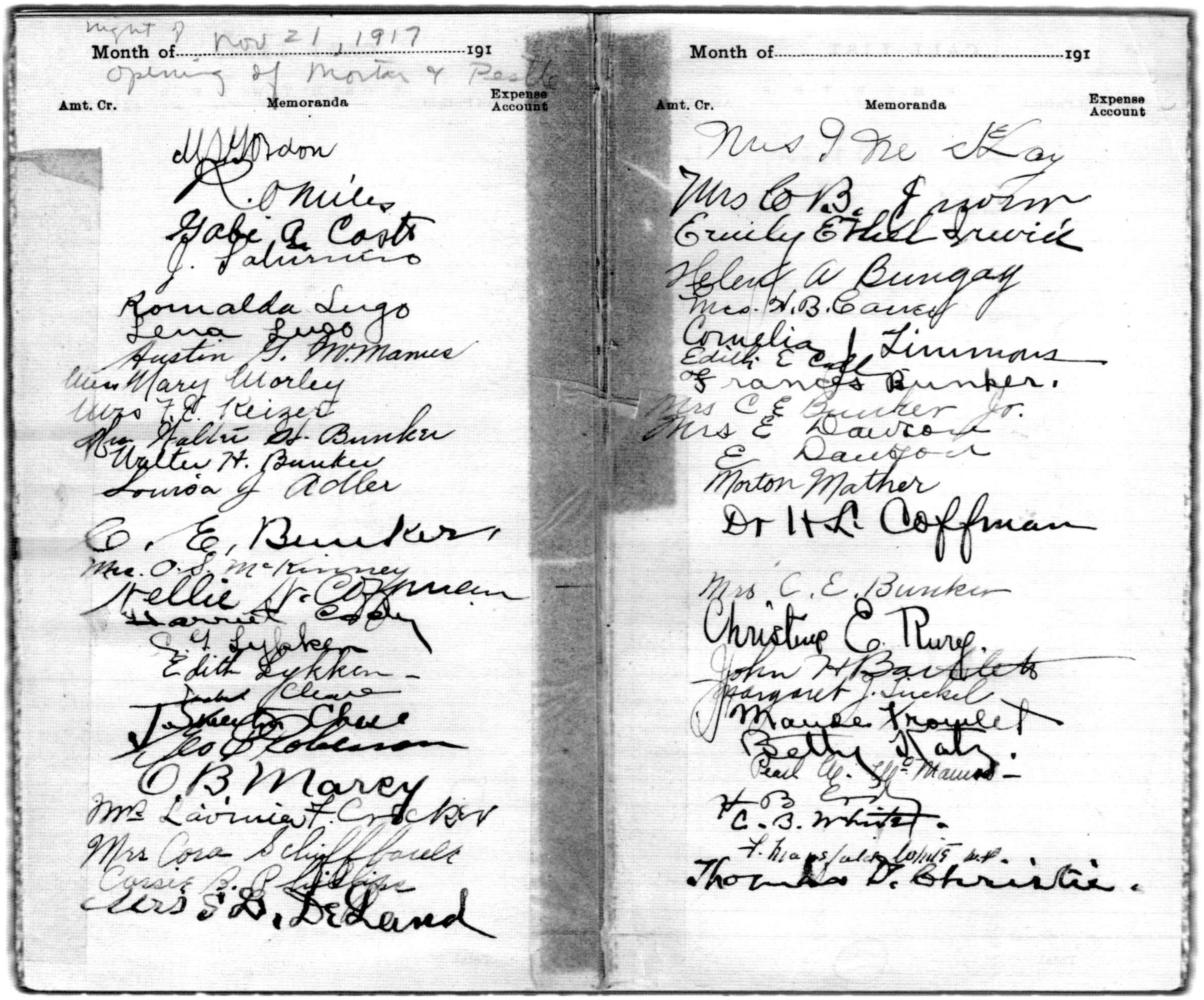

Month of Nov 21, 1917 191
Opening of Mortar & Pestle

Amt. Cr. | Memoranda | Expense Account

M. Gordon
R. O. Miles
Gabe A. Costo
J. Saturnino
Romalda Lugo
Lena Lugo
Austin G. McManus
Mrs. Mary Morley
Mrs. F. E. Keizer
Mrs. Walter H. Bunker
Walter H. Bunker
Louisa J. Adler
C. E. Bunker
Mrs. O. S. McKinney
Nellie N. Coffman
Harriet Coffman
E. T. Lykken
Edith Lykken
[illegible] Chase
J. Smeaton Chase
Geo. Robinson
O. B. Marcy
Mrs. Lavinia F. Crocker
Mrs. Cora Schiffbauer
Cossie B. Phillips
Mrs. S. D. DeLand

Month of 191

Amt. Cr. | Memoranda | Expense Account

Mrs. I. McKay
Mrs. C. B. Eaton
Emily Ethel Irwick
Helen A. Bungay
Mrs. H. B. Carey
Cornelia J. Timmons
Edith E. Coff
Frances Bunker
Mrs. C. E. Bunker Jr.
Mrs. E. Dawson
E. Dawson
Morton Mather
Dr. H. L. Coffman
Mrs. C. E. Bunker
Christine E. Rure
John H. Bartlett
Margaret J. Tickel
Maude Krouplet
Betty Katz
Pearl W. McManus
H. B. [illegible]
C. B. White
[illegible]
Thomas D. Christie

INDEX TO GREAT REGISTER OF PALM SPRINGS PRECINCT

No.	Name	Occupation	Party Affiliation	P. O. Address
1	Adler, Mrs. Louise J.	Hotel Keeper	Republican	Palm Springs, California
2	Adler, Otto E.	Merchant	Republican	" "
3	Bunker, Chauncey E., Jr.	Garage Man	Declines	" "
4	Bunker, Chauncey E., Sr.	Real Estate	Republican	" "
5	Bunker, Mrs. Cynthia A.	Housewife	Democrat	" "
6	Bunker, Mrs. Ursula	Housewife	Democrat	" "
7	Bunker, Walter H.	Machinist	Democrat	" "
8	Bunker, Mrs. Zadie R.	Housewife	Prohibition	" "
9	Christie, Thomas D.	Pastor	Republican	" "
10	Coffman, Harry L.	Physician	Republican	" "
11	Coffman, Mrs. Helen A.	Housewife	Republican	" "
12	Coffman, Mrs. Nellie N.	Inn Keeper	Democrat	" "
13	Coffman, Owen E.	Hotel Clerk	Democrat	" "
14	Crocker, Mrs. Lavina F.	Housewife	Republican	" "
15	Da Vall, Everett K.	Farmer	Republican	" "
16	Da Vall, Mrs. Grace H.	Housewife	Republican	" "
17	De Land, Mrs. Sarah L.	Housewife	Republican	" "
18	Demuth, A.	Carpenter	Declines	" "
19	Diepold, Carl	Laborer	Republican	" "
20	Gentry, Josiah	Laborer	Democrat	" "
21	Gordon, M. S.	Farmer	Declines	" "
22	Gray, James A.	Merchant	Republican	" "
23	Gray, Mrs. Jennie	Inn Keeper	Republican	" "
24	Hoffman, Daniel	Laborer	Democrat	" "
25	Keizer, Fred E	Retired	Republican	" "
26	Kocher, Mrs. Clareta M.	Housewife	Republican	" "
27	Kocher, Jacob John	Physician & Surgeon	Republican	" "
28	Lewis, Mrs. Lavina	Housekeeper	Democrat	" "
29	Lykken, Carl G.	Postmaster	Republican	" "
30	Lykken, Mrs. Edith C.	Housewife	Republican	" "
31	McKinney, Oliver S.	Farmer	Democrat	" "
32	McKinney, Mrs. Rosa M.	Housewife	Republican	" "
33	McManus, Austin G.	Real Estate Agent	Democrat	" "
34	Patton, Henry H.	Plumber	Republican	" "
35	Randles, James L.	Hotel-Keeper	Democrat	" "
36	Randles, John F.	Hotelman	Democrat	" "
37	Rury, Miss Christine E.	School Teacher	Republican	" "
38	Stevens, Mrs. Frances Stephens	Housewife	Democrat	" "
39	White, Miss Cornelia	Housekeeper	Declines	" "
40	White, Miss Florilla M.	Housekeeper	Republican	" "

Election 1918.

The Palm Springs voting register of 1918 listed forty names.

PALM SPRINGS HISTORICAL SOCIETY COLLECTION

RIGHT: Election day in Palm Springs at the most logical polling place, The Desert Inn. *Far right:* Dr. Harry Coffman; Carl Eytel sits in front of him. Zaddie Bunker, in the white dress, is seated at the center table.

PALM SPRINGS HISTORICAL SOCIETY COLLECTION

LEFT: Willie Pablo was the law on the Agua Caliente Reservation. Though his home was in the pass on the Morongo Reservation, he spent considerable time in Palm Springs, often joining the cook at The Desert Inn to watch preparations in the outdoor kitchen near one of the tent houses. Photo taken about 1913.

PALM SPRINGS HISTORICAL SOCIETY COLLECTION

In 1907, Raymond Cree became the County of Riverside's superintendent of schools. When he moved to Palm Springs in 1920, he started growing dates. His date palms still produce today, and can be seen near Cree Road in Cathedral City.

PHOTO BY FRANK BOGERT

Raymond Cree

Raymond Cree was Superintendent of Schools for Riverside County from 1907 to 1920. A frequent Palm Springs visitor, he moved to the village in 1920 on sixty-five acres of land he had purchased five years earlier in Section 29, near the eastern city limit. After serving in France in World War I, he returned and started growing dates, hired Oliver McKinney to dig two wells, and built an adobe ranch house. The original Palm Valley School, later King's School, was part of his ranch and many of the original date palms continue to produce.

By 1946, Cree owned considerable land in the valley, including a section he sold to Frank Bogert for $34,000, which later became the site of the Thunderbird Country Club. He remained active in real estate until his death at age 87. The Raymond Cree Middle School in Palm Springs is named in his memory.

The first Indian Catholic Church in Palm Springs was located on Section 14, at the intersection of Calle El Segundo and Arenas Road. The older tribal members were very upset when the name of the church was changed from St. Florian's Chapel to Our Lady of Guadalupe. The original name honored Fr. Florian Hahn, director of St. Boniface School in Banning.

PALM SPRINGS HISTORICAL SOCIETY COLLECTION

John and Freda Miller stayed at the Palm Springs Hotel in 1921. Struck by the wonderful winter climate, John made an offer on the Monte Vista Apartments. His wife tried to stop the deal, but his offer was accepted and the Millers became village property owners. The following year they returned to Palm Springs with their sons, Frank and John. For the next sixty-five years, the Millers ran the property as a hotel, the city's oldest continuously operated business. Frank served for eight years on the City Council during the time Charlie Farrell was mayor. John also served twenty-one years on the Planning Commission, six years on the Architectural Commission, three years on the Redevelopment Commission, on the Historic Site Commission and the Board of the Historical Society. John was a noted collector and respected authority on western art.

PHOTOS COURTESY JOHN MILLER
PALM SPRINGS HISTORICAL SOCIETY COLLECTION

LEFT: Miss Katherine Finchy was one of two new Palm Springs teachers who arrived in 1922. She eventually became principal of Frances Stevens School and superintendent of the Desert School District. Katherine retired in 1951 after twenty-nine years in the field of education.

PALM SPRINGS HISTORICAL SOCIETY COLLECTION

BELOW: Palm Springs' first school district was founded in 1893 and the first schoolhouse was erected in 1895. It was located at what is now Indian Canyon Drive and Amado Road. Welwood Murray is credited with inducing the Southern Pacific Railroad's local authorities to build the little wooden schoolhouse. It was the only school in town until P.T. Stevens, developer of the El Mirador Hotel, donated land for a new elementary school. In 1927, the first rooms of the new building were completed and named the Frances Stevens School. The building remains as a historic site. It is located on North Palm Canyon Drive at Alejo Road. The first high school students were enrolled in the new Palm Springs High School on Ramon Road in 1938, ending the need for students to travel to Banning. Raymond Cree was appointed the first president of the Palm Springs Union High School District.

PALM SPRINGS HISTORICAL SOCIETY COLLECTION

Katherine Finchy

Perhaps the most influential woman in the history of education in Palm Springs was Miss Katherine Finchy. A young school teacher from Wabasha, Minnesota, Katherine arrived by train at Whitewater Station on a fall day in 1922 and was transported to her new home at Palm Springs by buckboard. That night, the town entertained their new teacher at a dance in Harry Mutascio's pool hall.

In 1893, Miss Annie Noble had been hired as the district's first teacher for a session lasting only six months. That school year there was a total of twenty-one students, thirteen Indians and eight white settlers.

Katherine was one of two teachers in 1922, having been preceded by at least twenty others who could not tolerate the loneliness and heat of the desert community. Miss Finchy eventually became principal of Frances Stevens School, and was later appointed the superintendent of the Desert School District. She retired in 1951 after twenty-nine years of service.

Besides her dedication to her profession, Katherine was always active in civic and religious affairs. Her favorite organization was the local branch of the Soroptimist Club, which she founded and served as charter president. She also organized Soroptimist clubs in Mexico, Cuba, Panama and Peru. She was dedicated to the Palm Springs Historical Society, serving as board member and volunteer coordinator until 1982.

Katherine Finchy died in 1986 at the age of ninety-four. After living in the desert valley for sixty-five years, she was a true desert girl.

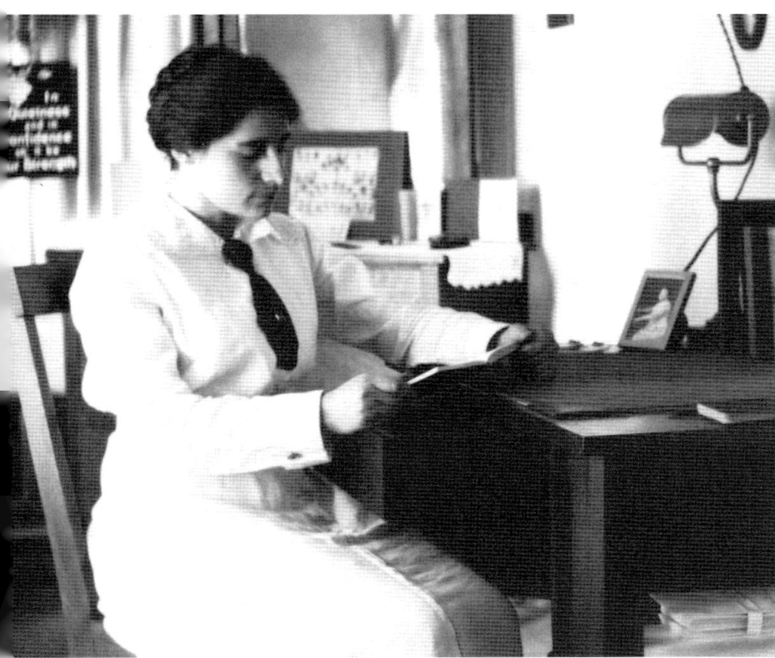

ABOVE: Preparing for her life as a school teacher, twenty-two year old Katherine Finchy studies at Biola University in Los Angeles.

PALM SPRINGS HISTORICAL SOCIETY COLLECTION

RIGHT: Harold Hicks, Palm Springs pioneer and former student of Katherine Finchy, presents her with a schoolhouse replica on her eighty-third birthday.

PHOTO BY GAIL THOMPSON

Rudolph Valentino, working on a French Foreign Legion movie in the desert about 1920, is entertained by William Pester, the hermit of Palm Springs.

PALM SPRINGS HISTORICAL SOCIETY COLLECTION

Mounting a horse was a little out of Rudolph Valentino's line, *at left*. He seems to have lost his head in an attempt to vault into the saddle without using the stirrups. Finally in the saddle, *at right*, Rudy looks composed and at ease. Perhaps he learned to ride when playing roles in other movies, like *The Sheik*.

PALM SPRINGS HISTORICAL SOCIETY COLLECTION

A motion picture company films near Tahquitz Canyon in 1923.

PALM SPRINGS DESERT MUSEUM COLLECTION

Movie-making in the early days of Palm Springs. The cameramen shoot a scene in an early William Fox Western. Notice the old Concord stagecoach (c. 1919).

PALM SPRINGS HISTORICAL SOCIETY COLLECTION

Villagers turn out to watch a movie being made at The Desert Inn in 1922.

PHOTO BY HUMPHREY BIRGE, COURTESY CAROLINE BIRGE SUMMERS (FACING CAMERA)

LEFT: In the 1920s, Fatty Arbuckle was one of Hollywood's most popular stars. He made several pictures in Palm Springs and spent several seasons at The Desert Inn.

PALM SPRINGS DESERT MUSEUM COLLECTION

RIGHT: Ernest Torrence became a star after his part in *Covered Wagon*. Here, Torrence comforts an unidentified actress in an African safari picture made in Palm Springs in 1923.

PALM SPRINGS HISTORICAL SOCIETY COLLECTION

ABOVE: Many movie companies filmed in the desert around Palm Springs in the 1920s. Here, Theda Bara and company shoot *Salome* in 1922.

PALM SPRINGS DESERT MUSEUM COLLECTION

Lawrence Crossley

Lawrence Crossley was hired by P.T. Stevens in New York. When he arrived in Palm Springs in 1924, he found himself to be one of the first black people living in the village. Born in New Orleans, he was taught to play the trumpet by Louis Armstrong and played regularly with several jazz bands in the French Quarter. After a month of living in the village, he decided to make Palm Springs his home, sending for his wife Martha and his two daughters, Margaret and Yvonne.

Lawrence soon became P.T. Stevens' right-hand man, receiving the title of Zanjero when he took over the operation of the Whitewater Mutual Water Company. He was one of the early investors in the El Mirador Hotel, built a golf course for Stevens, and after Stevens' death, continued to manage the water company. Well-liked by the Indians, he became an advisor to many Indian families, and, in later years, was appointed by Judge Hilton McCabe as a conservator for several Indians.

Crossley owned trailer parks, a private water company, a laundromat, a restaurant and the Crossley Courts on Ramon Road. He was a pilot, prospector, politician and businessman. He owned a company that packaged desert plants used by the Indians for a medicinal tea and a facial clay used by beauticians. Crossley developed the village he called Tramview, in Cathedral City, twenty years before the Tramway became a reality. He built the Crossley tract on twenty acres Pearl McManus traded in exchange for a Buick. The street to the Tahquitz Creek Golf Resort and his subdivision bears the name Crossley Road.

Lawrence and Martha were highly respected and well-liked by villagers. His beautiful daughters were very popular in the local high school. Both were married to wealthy Los Angeles businessmen.

Lawrence Crossley

Martha Crossley

PHOTOS COURTESY YVONNE CROSSLEY LOGGINS

Murray Lamb, an employee of Oliver S. McKinney, beside McKinney's REO truck about 1925. The palm was the first to be delivered to the home of Mr. and Mrs. King Gillette in Tahquitz Estates.

PALM SPRINGS HISTORICAL SOCIETY COLLECTION

In the 1920s, the Pierce Arrow was the finest car made in the United States. Humphrey Birge, whose father had been a major investor in the car company, always drove one. This photo was taken in the Sunshine Court where the Birges lived while building their estate at the corner of Belardo and Ramon Roads (the Ingleside Inn).

PHOTO COURTESY CAROLINE SUMMERS

Philip Boyd

Phil Boyd was primarily known as the first mayor of Palm Springs, but he made many other contributions to the city. He arrived in the desert in 1926 and was married at The Desert Inn to Dorothy B. Marmon of the Marmon Car Company in Indianapolis. Boyd managed the Palm Springs branch of the Bank of America from 1929 to 1934. After serving on the incorporation committee for two years, he was elected to the City Council in 1938 and served two years as mayor. In 1945 he was elected assemblyman, representing Riverside County in Sacramento.

He wrote the bill making construction of the Palm Springs Aerial Tramway possible and was instrumental in getting the University of California at Riverside established. His land investments included all of the Deep Well area from Sunrise Way west to the Biltmore area, which had formerly been Oliver S. McKinney's alfalfa farm. In his later years, he lived in Palm Desert near the ranch he donated to the Living Desert, close to land he gave for the University of California Desert Experimental Center in Deep Canyon.

Boyd served on the Board of Regents of the University of California and was a director of the Security First National Bank and Palm Springs Desert Museum. The Boyds had four children and several grandchildren.

Dorothy and Phil Boyd at the start of their honeymoon on March 10, 1926, stand by a borrowed Marmon car in the driveway of photographer Stephen Willard's home. Mrs. Boyd's family owned the Marmon Automobile Company. Mr. Boyd was later Palm Springs' first mayor.

PALM SPRINGS DESERT MUSEUM COLLECTION

Winter snowfall in January 1930, a rare event that occurs about once every ten years. The 1930 snowfall measured about four inches; the next morning it had melted. The photographer was standing in the 100 block of North Palm Canyon Drive. Compare Palm Springs' Main Street *(above)*, later Palm Canyon Drive, in 1930, with the quiet street fifteen years earlier *(below)* when a traveling photographer came to town, parking his unusual vehicle in front of the new Hotel La Palma. The hotel was built by Mr. and Mrs. Otto Adler with the help of local citizens. The Adlers came to Palm Springs in 1914, opening a grocery store in a tent and later buying the village's only fire apparatus. It was locked inside Ed Bunker's garage when the Adler's tent caught fire and burned to the ground. Their hostelry later became the El Rey, which in turn was razed and the famous Chi Chi erected. The site is in the 200 block of North Palm Canyon Drive.

PALM SPRINGS HISTORICAL SOCIETY COLLECTION

Rob Riddle ran the little dirt airport on Section 14 in Palm Springs in the 1930s. His "airline" consisted of a one-passenger plane that flew to Burbank.

PALM SPRINGS HISTORICAL SOCIETY COLLECTION

News of the arrival of New York's flamboyant mayor Jimmy Walker appeared in every newspaper in the United States. California Governor James "Sunny Jim" Rolph flew down from San Francisco with the city's mayor and famous racing pilot, Roscoe Turner. The plane belonged to Earl Gilmore, whose oil company was later absorbed by Mobil.

PHOTO BY TONY BURKE

The first plane to land on the dirt strip in Section 14 was the sister ship to Charles Lindbergh's Spirit of St. Louis. Piloting the plane in this 1928 landing was Bert Jacobson.

PALM SPRINGS HISTORICAL SOCIETY COLLECTION

In 1932 when Gary Cooper showed up at the stables dressed in jodhpurs and a beret, cowboys were shocked. They nearly fainted when "Coop" requested an English saddle! Cooper was born to a Montana ranch family, though, and knew his saddles.

PHOTO BY TONY BURKE

ABOVE: Julia S. Carnell, owner of the National Cash Register Company in Dayton, Ohio, visited Palm Springs in the winter of 1930. Returning in 1931, she bought the site on which the old Presbyterian Church had stood and built the biggest office building in town. It was so successful an enterprise that she bought Miss Cornelia White's three and one-half acres and built the Plaza, later owned by Zachary Pitts and Stanley Rosin. Robert Ransom, a local Realtor, engineered the deal, and architect Harry Williams was summoned from Dayton to design the property. Desmond's, a store from Los Angeles, opened in 1936, and within one year the entire project was rented. *Left to right:* Robert Ransom, unidentified woman, Mrs. Julia S. Carnell and Frank Bogert at the Desert Circus.

PALM SPRINGS HISTORICAL SOCIETY COLLECTION

RIGHT: Ed Fitzgerald was another of Palm Springs' hermits. He lived at "Green Tree," a group of trees in the Tahquitz Wash. Fitzgerald could be seen daily walking down Palm Canyon Drive in his usual garb – walking shorts, hat, and cane, sans shoes or shirt. It was rumored that he had once been a stockbroker and came to Palm Springs after the Wall Street crash. Ed suffered a heart attack while collecting golf balls at O'Donnell Golf Course; taken to Desert Hospital, he refused treatment and was later found dead at his little home in the riverbed.

PALM SPRINGS HISTORICAL SOCIETY COLLECTION

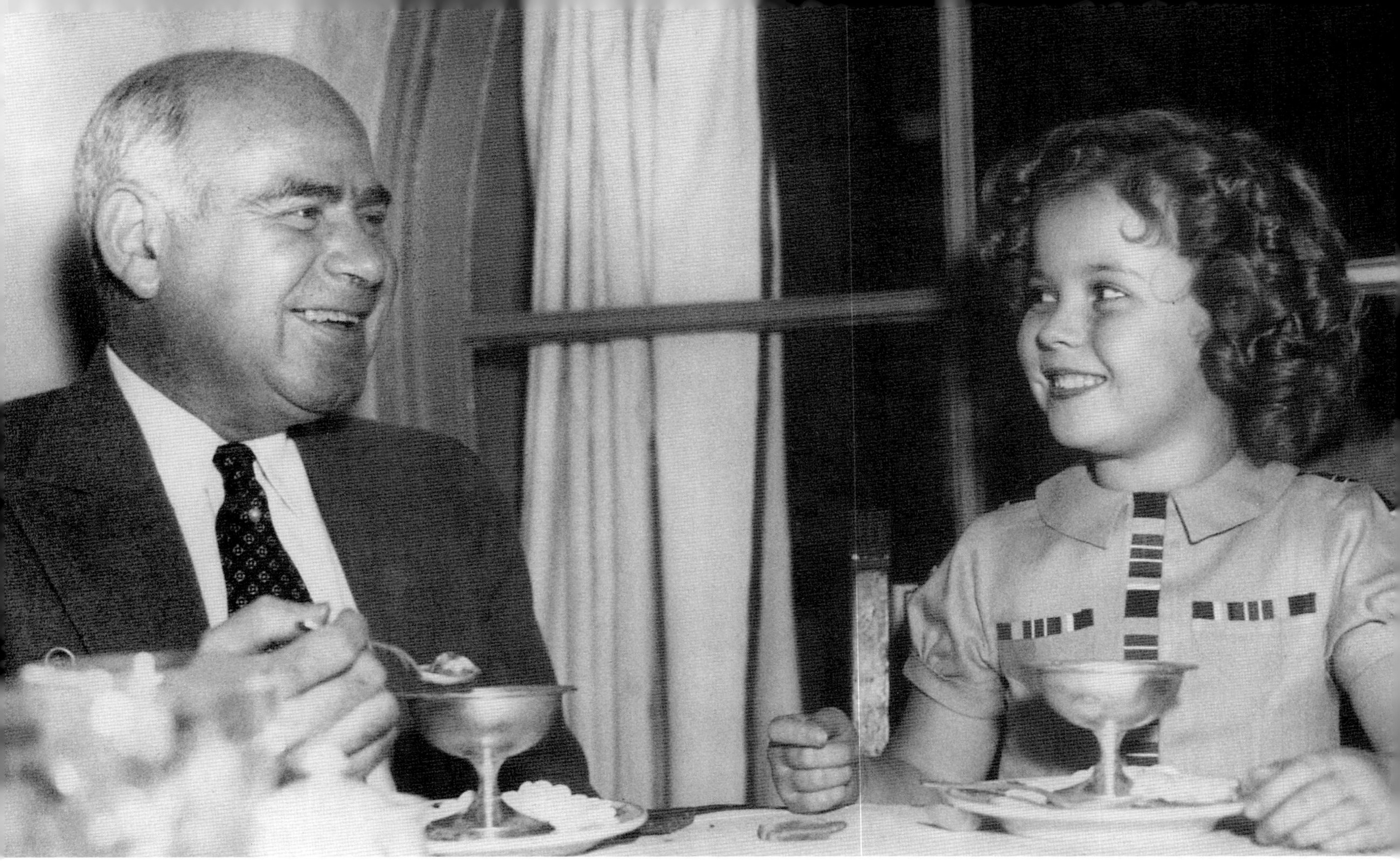

Shirley Temple and her family were frequent guests at The Desert Inn in the 1930s. During one of their visits, Herbert Lehman, governor of New York, was also in town, staying at the El Mirador. He absolutely refused to allow anyone to take his picture, but he told the author that the one person in the world he wanted to meet was Shirley Temple. After calling Shirley's mother and arranging a luncheon for the governor and the star, the author asked the governor if he would like a photograph with Shirley. His response was "please do." Of the twelve pictures taken, this shot of the two of them eating ice cream was the only good one. Shirley set up the photograph; she had the governor look a little to the right and she cheated to the left; the results appeared in twelve hundred newspapers and six magazines!

PHOTO BY FRANK BOGERT

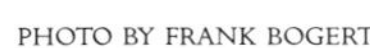

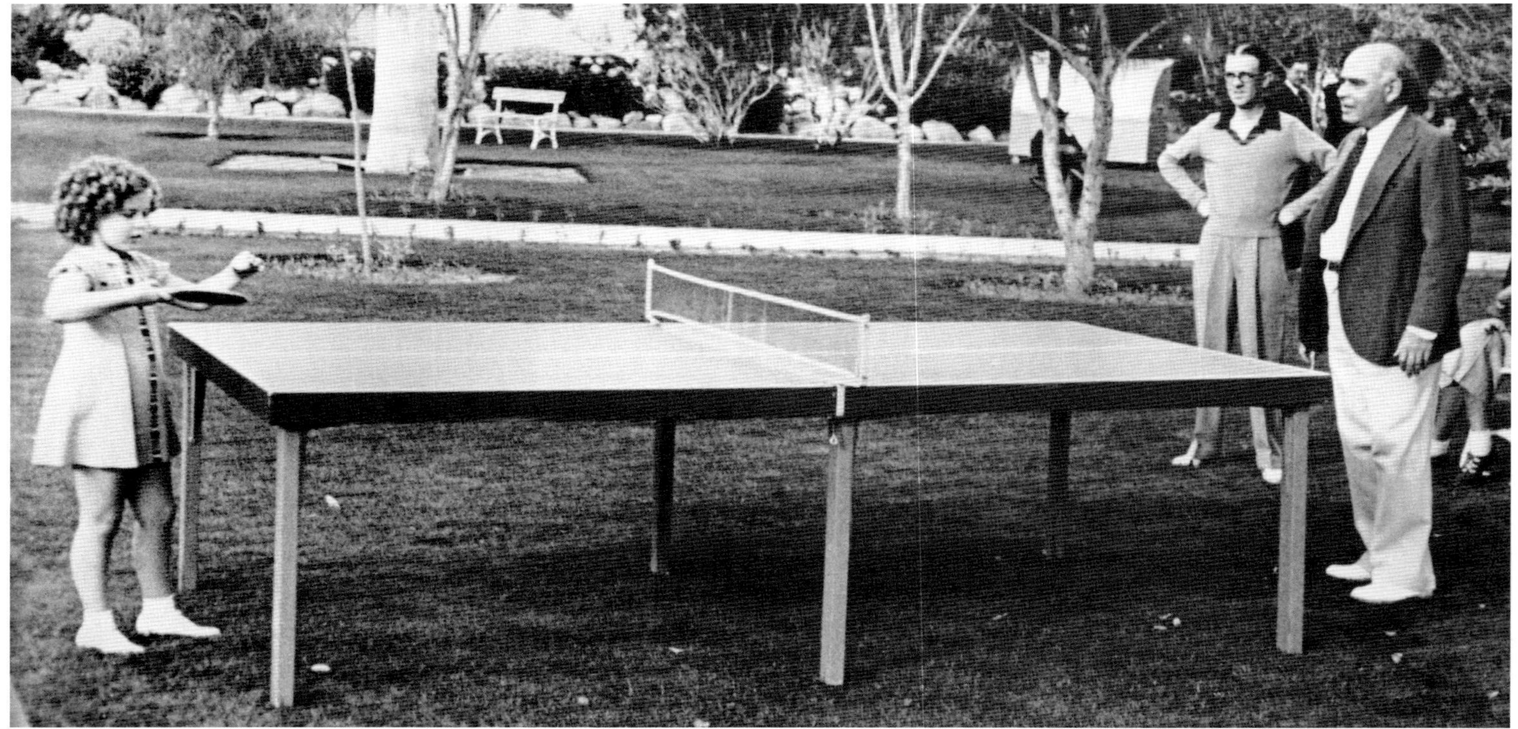

ABOVE: Warren Pinney, *right*, an attorney with the firm of O'Melveny & Myers in Los Angeles, assumed management of the El Mirador Hotel for the bondholders in 1932. Soon recognized as one of the country's top resort hotelmen, he was one of the village's leading citizens. In 1942, the federal government purchased the hotel from Pinney and his partner, Ralph Lacoe, and transformed it into Torney General Hospital, a facility for wounded soldiers from the South Pacific front. When the war ended, it was sold as surplus and opened again in 1952 with its former reputation for glamour intact. He is shown here in 1933 with one of the earliest nationally known figures to visit Palm Springs, Samuel Untermyer, a New York attorney. Untermyer later owned an estate named "The Willows" on West Tahquitz Canyon Way in back of The Desert Inn.

PHOTO BY FRANK BOGERT

LEFT & FACING PAGE BOTTOM: After lunch and a three-hour talk, Shirley and Governor Lehman played a game of ping pong. The author was the assistant manager and publicist for the El Mirador and all the pictures he had taken that day bore the name of that hotel. Earl Coffman called the next day, extremely irate that Shirley had publicized the El Mirador, when, in fact, she was staying at The Desert Inn.

PHOTO BY FRANK BOGERT

Mr. and Mrs. Adolph Spreckles, a San Francisco couple from the well-known sugar family, are photographed in 1932 by Tony Burke, the El Mirador's first publicity man.

PHOTO BY TONY BURKE

LEFT: In 1932, the only tennis courts in town were at the El Mirador Hotel and The Desert Inn. Claudette Colbert is shown serving at the El Mirador court.

PHOTO BY FRANK BOGERT

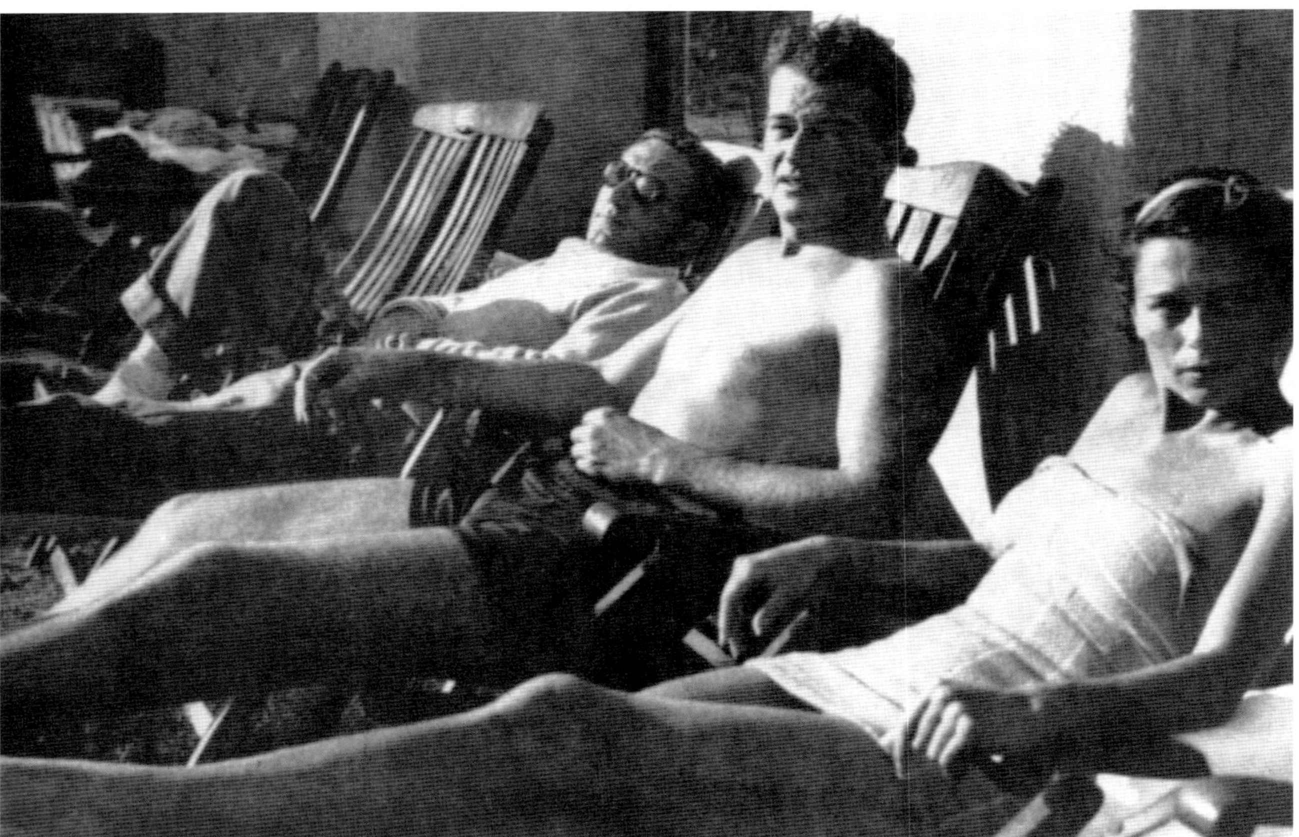

Relaxing poolside at the El Mirador Hotel in 1931 are Spencer Tracy and Mr. and Mrs. John Wayne.

PALM SPRINGS HISTORICAL SOCIETY COLLECTION

Tony Burke knew little about photography when he took the job at the El Mirador in 1932. He soon learned that showing subjects walking made them look less posed. *Left to right:* Lionel Barrymore; his wife, Renee Fenwick; Dolores Costello; and her husband, John Barrymore.

PHOTO BY TONY BURKE

BELOW: Actress Paulette Goddard, British author H.G. Wells, and Charlie Chaplin's three children are shown at the El Mirador Hotel. Paulette, secretly married to Chaplin, was a frequent guest of the hotel in the 1930s.

PHOTO BY TONY BURKE

Mr. and Mrs. Buddy Rogers were frequent winter guests in Palm Springs. Mrs. Rogers, Mary Pickford, is seen here with Frank Bogert at the El Mirador Hotel.

PHOTO BY GAIL THOMPSON

Earle Strebe was a civic leader in Palm Springs for many years.

PALM SPRINGS HISTORICAL SOCIETY COLLECTION

Earle Strebe

Earle Strebe came to the valley around 1927 and worked as a bellman in Nellie Coffman's hotel. He was often asked to show movies to the guests at The Desert Inn and soon the management of the Oasis Hotel also asked him to show films. As his reputation as a projectionist grew, he began his own business, presenting movies at Frances Stevens School, with Katherine Finchy collecting tickets.

Earle married Zaddie Bunker's daughter Frances, who had just graduated from osteopathic school. With Zaddie's assistance, he built the Village Theater in addition to helping Zaddie handle her properties in Palm Springs. Earle was always one of the village leaders; he worked on the first Desert Circus, headed the Chamber of Commerce, and twice was elected to the Palm Springs City Council.

In 1938 no bridge stood at Araby Point, where the Palm Canyon Wash crosses Highway 111. The pavement washed out that year during one of the century's worst floods. Road graders spent more time pulling automobiles out of the sand than they did in restoring the roadway.

PHOTO BY FRANK BOGERT

Owners George (brother of Earle) and Ethel Strebe and two bovine friends at The Doll House during Desert Circus week in 1950.

PHOTO COURTESY PEG STANS RASHALL

For many years The Doll House was perhaps the most popular restaurant and night spot in Palm Springs. The Guadalajara Trio played in the bar and the steaks, special Doll House potatoes and hot sweet rolls won accolades. After a party, almost everyone ended up at The Doll House.

PHOTO BY GAIL THOMPSON

Clara Bow, the "It Girl," was Hollywood's leading sex symbol in the 1930s. Clara and her husband Rex Bell spent a considerable amount of time at their home in the village. Clara is shown here with Frank Bogert on the patio of Chuck Morrison's home in 1935.

PHOTO BY REX BELL

Mary Astor, one of Hollywood's most beautiful stars, lived at her home in the desert foothills. She is seen here with actor Frank Morgan at the Rogers Ranch.

PHOTO BY FRANK BOGERT

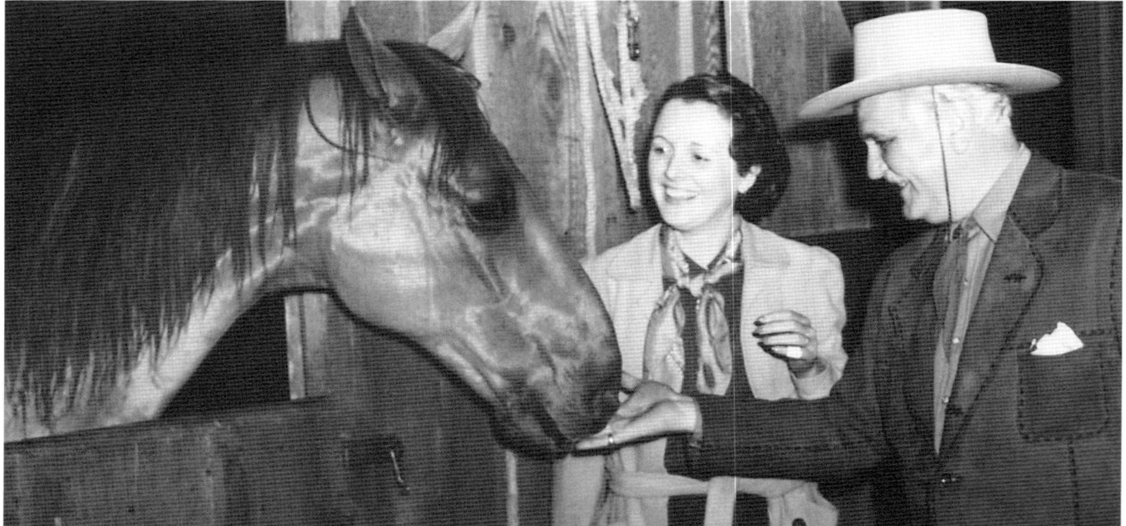

Cathedral City was a small village about one mile in length on either side of Highway 111 in 1935. Incorporated in 1981, it now contains almost twenty square miles.

RAY JONES COLLECTION

On November 30, 1938, NBC stars turned out en masse to help open the winter season of the El Mirador Hotel. Photo shows stars of Amos 'n Andy radio show watching a swimming meet at the outdoor pool as the season's first cold wave hits Eastern states. *Left to right, seated:* Freeman (Amos) Gosden, Macaline (Genevieve Blue) Lee, Charles (Andy) Correll. *Back row:* Helen Wood and Marion Talley.

PHOTO BY FRANK BOGERT

ABOVE: The first Desert Circus was held in Palm Springs in 1934 to raise money for the church rectory on the Agua Caliente Reservation. The Kangaroo Court was held on the grounds of The Desert Inn. Culprits without western clothes were brought before Judge Warren Pinney. He levied fines ranging from ten dollars to one hundred dollars, all of which went to the church. Among the early villagers in this photo are Dutch Smith, Ernie and Emma Fors, Dr. Wesley Grey, Austin McManus, Earl Love, Little Bear, Ernie McDonald, Johnny Boyle, John Gardner, Frank Bennett, Robert Ransom, Frank Pershing, Ralph Marvin, Leslie Charteris, Irwin Schuman, George Gannon, Earl Gibbs, Lou Bramlett, Priscilla Chaffey, Lola Hotaling, Alvah Hicks, Milt Hicks, Tony Burke, Barney Hinkle, Mary Murphy, Frank Bogert, Mary Grabiner and her sister Helen, Bill Kidson, Dr. Henry Hoagland and Harriet Henderson.

FRANK BOGERT COLLECTION

BELOW: Melba Bennett staged a show each year for the Desert Circus, called Village Insanities. The one held in 1935 was on The Desert Inn grounds. Later shows were performed in the Plaza Theater.

PALM SPRINGS HISTORICAL SOCIETY COLLECTION

ABOVE: Winna O'Bear, known as Little Bear, worked as a desert equestrian guide for over twenty years. She bought a flag and assumed a position ahead of the Grand Marshal in the annual Desert Circus parade. It finally became a tradition; for the last six years of her life this well-known personality led every parade.

PHOTO BY JOHN MILLER

BELOW: By 1947, when this group was photographed, The Desert Circus was the biggest event of the season. Trav Rogers, the man in the white hat next to the clown, was the "High Sheriff" and the girls were his deputies. It was an honor to be chosen to sell badges and arrest people not dressed in western attire. When arrested, the prisoners had to appear before the judge at Kangaroo Court and pay fines. Judge for the 1946 event was Leo Fields, standing in the top row in a black hat.

PHOTO BY GAIL THOMPSON

LEFT: In 1936, when Ruth Hardy converted Carrie Birge's home into the Ingleside Inn, she retained most of the priceless furnishings, including an antique bed supposedly slept in by Queen Isabella. It became one of the city's most exclusive hotels. Owned and operated later by Mel Haber, the restaurant on the grounds is called Melvyn's.

PHOTO BY STEPHEN WILLARD, PALM SPRINGS HISTORICAL SOCIETY COLLECTION

ABOVE: Edgar Bergen was overcome when presented in 1938 with a tiny western saddle for Charlie McCarthy by the rodeo committee at Rogers Stables.

PHOTO BY FRANK BOGERT

ABOVE: An Indian pageant staged in Palm Canyon in 1938 featured performances by over one hundred Hollywood "Indians." Starlet June Travis was on hand for a publicity shot.

PHOTO BY FRANK BOGERT

RIGHT: June Travis, Warner Brothers' starlet, had just completed her role in *Ceiling Zero*, also staring James Cagney. June's real name was Grabiner; the name "Travis" came from Travis Rogers, shown here with June at his stables.

PHOTO BY FRANK BOGERT

ABOVE: Frank Bennett arrived in Palm Springs in the 1930s. Frank and his wife Melba were managers and part-owners of Deep Well Ranch and later became involved in almost every city activity. Frank was on the first incorporation committee. Melba ran the Village Insanities and was the founder of the Palm Springs Historical Society in 1955. When a dude ranch opened in competition with Deep Well, Frank helped to make the new venture successful.

PHOTO BY GAIL THOMPSON

For many years, Dr. Henry Hoagland was president of the Desert Riders, Palm Springs' oldest horse and riding club. He was president of the Desert Circus in 1939 when this photograph was taken and served on the city incorporation committee in 1937.

PHOTO BY FRANK BOGERT

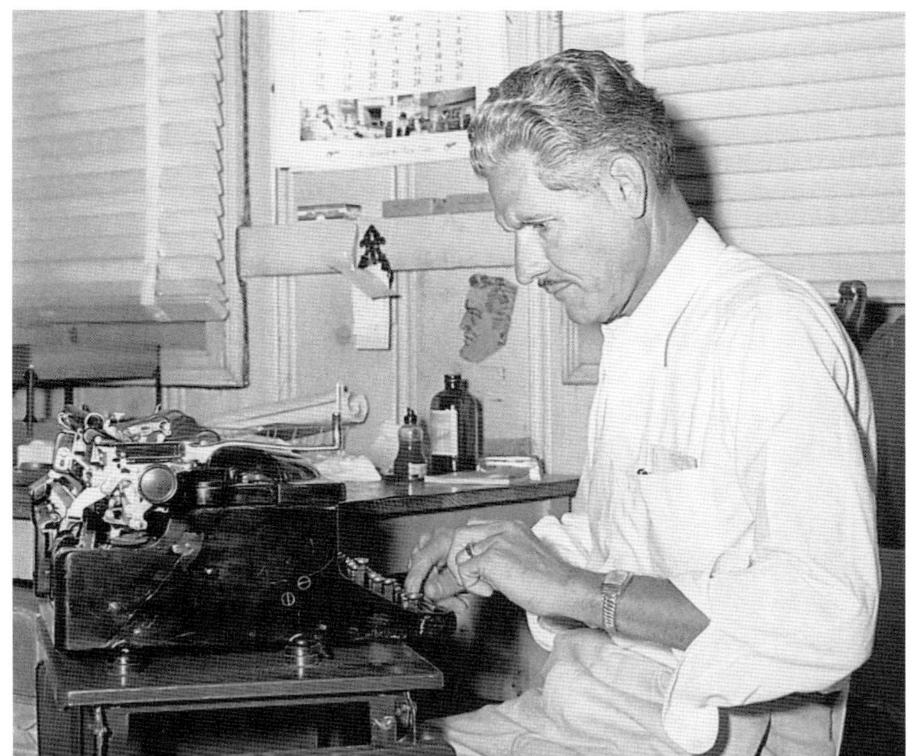

Oliver Jaynes, publisher of *The Desert Sun.* In 1949, Jaynes was president and founder of Palm Springs' first federal loan company, a business that was later to become the Santa Fe Federal.

PHOTO COURTESY PEG STANS EASHALL

Jim Maynard was one of Palm Springs' most colorful characters. He grew up in the city and was on the police force for several years. His 285 pounds of solid muscle made his mere presence a great deterrent to crime in the village.

PALM SPRINGS HISTORICAL SOCIETY COLLECTION

Janice Bogert, whose mother, Ruth Bibo, owned the Acoma Indian Store, models an Indian costume in 1947.

PHOTO BY FRANK BOGERT, PALM SPRINGS HISTORICAL SOCIETY COLLECTION

A great friend of the Indians, Jim Maynard *(left)* learned much about their culture. He was often called upon for rescue missions in the mountains because of his familiarity with the area. Maynard took the first engineers up the mountain to survey the Palm Springs Aerial Tramway.

PHOTO CIRCA 1941 BY GAIL THOMPSON

Writer, artist, museum curator and entrepreneur Cabot Yerxa built this structure in 1941 as a monument to the Indian people. Fashioned after a Hopi Indian pueblo, it was four stories high and contained thirty-five rooms, sixty-five doors, and one hundred and fifty windows. Yerxa, shown standing in front of his museum and home, died on March 5, 1965. Although he had worked on the pueblo for twenty-three years, it was not completed at the time of his death. Today Cabot's Old Indian Pueblo in Desert Hot Springs is open to the public.

PHOTO BY FRANK BOGERT

In 1947, Charlie Tanner took over the El Mirador Garage, which had been built to house valet parking for the hotel. He installed gas pumps and established Gray Line Tours. The twenty-four-passenger tallyho was used for sightseeing tours. The El Mirador Garage, at the southeast corner of Tachevah and North Palm Canyon Drives, was later renovated and has served variously as an art gallery and medical offices.

PHOTO COURTESY PEG STANS RASHALL

PALM SPRINGS

Palm Springs' own movie starlet, June Travis, is shown in a shot by Scottie Welborn, the famous Hollywood photographer. The Palm Springs sign on the board and "one leg up" pose were typical of the cheesecake photography of the time. June was the daughter of Harry Grabiner, manager of the Chicago White Sox ball team. She was discovered in Palm Springs by Hal Wallis and given a contract at Warner Brothers Studio. Her first picture was *Ceiling Zero* costarring James Cagney; her second was a movie featuring Ronald Reagan in his first film. June was the sweetheart of Palm Springs, queen of the Desert Circus and Rodeo Queen. She lived over twenty years in Palm Springs with her family.

PHOTO BY SCOTTIE WELBORN

4

Fifty Golden Years

As Palm Springs grew, it soon became apparent that the village needed zoning restrictions and other types of controls. In November 1936, a committee to study incorporation was formed with Frank Bennett as temporary chairman. On the thirty-man committee were Earl Coffman, Fred Markham, Warren Pinney, Alvah Hicks, Ralph Bellamy, Phil Boyd, Culver Nichols and Jack Williams.

Harold Hicks, selected as the permanent committee chairman, called a meeting on August 14, 1937, to finalize city boundaries, divide the area into seven wards and draw up an incorporation petition to be signed by property owners. After a number of discussions with the county, the incorporation matter came to a vote on April 1, 1938. Not all of the town's 910 registered voters turned out; the final tally was 442 in favor of incorporation, 211 against.

A very vocal opposition attempted to petition against incorporation, but to no avail. Seven councilmen, one from each ward, were elected: Austin G. McManus, John W. Williams, Frank Shannon, Philip L. Boyd, Alvah Hicks, Robert Murray and Dr. Bacon Cliffton. Boyd was selected as the city's first mayor. Other city officials were Guy Pinney (Warren's brother), City Clerk; Roy Colgate, City Attorney; Fred Ingram, City Treasurer; Lloyd Boller, Chief of Police and Bill Leonesio, Fire Chief.

Under the guidance of Mayor Boyd, a very capable businessman, the new city began with a solid financial foundation. A 1939 census numbered 5,336 year-round residents with a seasonal jump to over 8,000 people.

The city's four large hotels (The El Mirador, The Desert Inn, the Del Tahquitz and the Oasis) and the Deep Well Guest Ranch were packed during the season, encouraging the construction of many smaller hostelries. Irwin Schuman's Chi Chi became a full-scale nightclub, attracting nationally-known performers. Among the other leading restaurants were Vic Sudaha's popular Palm House, the Foldesy family's Polynesian restaurant in the Palm Springs Hotel and George and Ethel Strebe's Doll House. Trav Rogers started a western nightspot appropriately called "The Mink and Manure Club."

LEFT: Golden blooms of encilia and beavertail cactus cover the foothills of Palm Springs in the spring.

PHOTO BY GEORGE SERVICE

The Chi Chi was started by Irwin Schuman in 1936. He bought the restaurant from Jack Freeman and enlarged the operation every year until he occupied one-quarter of the 100 block of North Palm Canyon Drive. The Chi Chi was located on the site of the old La Palma Hotel, which later became the site of the Desert Fashion Plaza. Headliners who performed at the club included Patti Page, Sophie Tucker, Edgar Bergen, Peggy Lee, Dorothy Shay, Nat King Cole, Frank Sinatra, Lena Horne and Sammy Davis, Jr. (c. 1947)

PHOTO BY GAIL THOMPSON

Hollywood's film colony and tourists from all parts of the country discovered the desert playground. Palm Springs was in its heyday.

Among the wealth of outdoor activities were nine stables, Tom O'Donnell's golf course and several tennis courts including Charlie Farrell's prestigious Racquet Club. The city boasted more swimming pools than any other place in the country. Bicycle rentals were available at every hotel, and a bowling alley opened in the center of town. Everyone went to Cathedral City to gamble at Al Wertheimer's Dunes Club, Earl Sausser's 139 Club or Frank Portnoy's Cove Club.

On December 7, 1941, people crowded around the Mashie Course at The Desert Inn for the annual dog show heard John Miller announce that Pearl Harbor had been bombed. After the declaration of war, a few people left town in a panic; those who stayed prospered.

Palm Springs was filled with soldiers and visiting families. Torney General Hospital and the U.S. Ferry Command turned the village into a year-round resort. Although food rationing was a handicap to many hotels and restaurants, customers were satisfied.

On Sunday, December 7, 1941, The Desert Inn's Mashie Course was the scene of an annual dog show. Just as the setter class was being judged, Johnny Miller arrived to announce the bombing of Pearl Harbor.

PHOTO BY FRANK BOGERT

Nightlife, however, was a bit limited because of the blackout. (A little known, but interesting, piece of history: Torney General Hospital housed a large number of Italian war prisoners who worked as orderlies and at other jobs around the facility. A happy lot, they had been taken prisoner in the Tunisian campaign and were thoroughly adjusted to the desert climate.)

During World War II, the social leaders of the city served as Red Cross volunteers helping nurse the wounded at Torney General Hospital. These Red Cross Gray Ladies are Juanita Crockett, Dorothy Boyd and Harriet Henderson, mother of Joe Henderson, one of the city's prominent citizens.

PALM SPRINGS HISTORICAL SOCIETY COLLECTION

When peace was declared, tourists returned in even greater numbers; the village was back to normal. Although the need for additional housing was immediately recognized, it took two years for building materials to become readily available. The first new housing was started in the Veterans' Tract, east of El Cielo Road. Two million board feet of scarce timber caught fire on the site in 1946, causing the largest fire in the city's history. Though Bill Leonesio and his small staff did a grand job of trying to control the fire, Frank Broes was the hero of the day when he

The first City Council, elected in 1938. *Left to right:* Austin McManus, Jack Williams, Frank Shannon, Mayor Philip Boyd, Alvah F. Hicks, Robert Murray and Dr. Bacon Cliffton. After being elected to a second four-year term on the city council, Frank Shannon, owner of Vaughan Arms Apartments, was chosen by the council as mayor from 1942 to 1944.

PHOTO COURTESY JOHN MILLER

The Lucas sisters, trick riders from Bartlesville, Oklahoma, who spent the winter working at the Thunderbird Ranch, are pictured with Janice Bogert, late wife of Frank Bogert who was then managing owner of the ranch. *Left to right:* Sharon Lucas, Shirley Lucas and Janice Bogert.
FRANK BOGERT COLLECTION

brought in a bulldozer and cut a firebreak. Half of the precious lumber was saved, but the project was delayed for six months.

By 1947, Thunderbird Ranch, a new high school (originally opened in 1938), and several other buildings had been completed. Bullock's Wilshire had opened its large store on Palm Canyon Drive, and Paul Trousdale, in partnership with Pearl McManus, had built over two hundred homes in the Tahquitz River Estates. Almost six hundred thousand dollars in building permits were issued during the year for projects within the city limits.

Other towns not yet incorporated in the county also were prospering. Desert Hot Springs added a new spa, Cathedral City built new houses and a fire station, A. Ronald Button and John Culver started a new subdivision in Rancho Mirage and Cliff Henderson's undertaking across from the small community of Palm Village, later Palm Desert, was the valley's biggest project.

Edgar Bergen, who had a ranch east of Thunderbird, talked Cliff and his brother Randall into developing the 1,600 acres used by General Patton's tank repair facility during the war. Cliff formed Palm Desert Corporation, with Bergen and Leonard Firestone listed among the directors. Firecliff Lodge and the Shadow Mountain Club, several office buildings and a few homes were built. Thirty years later this area would become the city of Palm Desert.

The decade's other big event was the arrival of Avak the Faith Healer, who came to town to cure Krikor Arakelian's son. For weeks in May 1947, the town was filled to capacity with invalids seeking a miracle. Every newspaper in the country covered the story, but no cures were reported.

The city's press coverage continued when Charlie Farrell was selected by the City Council

Avak Hakopian was brought to Palm Springs in 1947 by a wealthy villager named Krikor Arakelian, who lived on Tamarisk Road across from the present Ruth Hardy Park. Avak had become famous as a healer, and Arakelian had a son afflicted from birth with an incurable ailment. Newspapers all over the country soon carried the story, and thousands of afflicted people descended on the town. The streets were jammed with cars, and a line of people waited outside the house daily. When Arakelian's son showed no improvement after a couple of months, Avak left and the village returned to normal.

PHOTO BY GAIL THOMPSON

to be its fifth mayor and the first to serve a five-year term. During his tenure as mayor, the television series *My Little Margie* starring Charlie and Gale Storm, was aired, making Farrell the best-known mayor in the United States. To make sure that the city stayed in the news, Cliff Brown of McFadden and Eddie, a Los Angeles advertising firm, served as the city's public relations representative during the 1950s.

Brothers Irwin (who had operated the Chi Chi for many years) and Mark Schuman built the Riviera Hotel in 1956. With a large number of rooms and a big conference center, they created the city's first complete convention facility.

After many years of litigation, the El Mirador Hotel reopened in the fall of 1952. Roy Fitzgerald from Chicago and seventeen other investors formed the National Hotel Investors, Inc. and spent over two million dollars remodeling the hotel. When it opened, it was even more glamorous than it had been before the war.

Although people had tried for many years to lease the hot springs from the Indians, it wasn't until 1957 that Sam Banowit convinced the Tribal Council that he could build a bathhouse that would return an investment to them. The agreement stipulated that he relocate the palm trees, sacred to the Indians, to another site. Though he originally anticipated investing $200,000 in the project, the final cost was $1,800,000.

After negotiating the first ninety-nine-year lease,

Whenever possible, publicity photos had to include the El Mirador tower in the background. A Palm Springs trademark, it's shown here in a typical shot with a model on a bicycle.

PHOTO BY FRANK BOGERT

Charles Farrell was the mayor of Palm Springs from 1948 to 1954. In the council chambers from the left, are Tom Kieley, Ruth Hardy, Florian Boyd, City Clerk Louise McCarn, City Attorney Warren Slaughter, Mayor Farrell, Gordon Feekings, Bill Veith, Wally Waring and City Manager Russell Rink.

PHOTO COURTESY PEG STANS RASHALL

Banowit built the adjoining five-story Spa Hotel. The architect was William F. Cody. The tribe was to receive all the income from the hot springs, which, together with their canyons and cemetery, were lands allocated to individual tribal members. Thus, the historic mineral springs, from which the Indian tribe and the city derived their names, became a world-class spa.

Palm Springs High School (1938) on Ramon Road was a great drawing card to lure families to the desert as was the city library established in 1939. After a hospital district was formed and a hospital built in 1952, Palm Springs had all the facilities it needed, except for an airport. One of the first accomplishments of the city council elected in 1958 was the purchase of the airport on Section 18 from the local Indians. The U.S. Ferry Command, which had built concrete runways capable of handling any

Gussie Moran, tennis glamour girl of the 1950s, created quite a furor when the lace on her underpants showed a little below her shorts. This photograph was taken at the Racquet Club, where she was frequently seen on the courts.

PALM SPRINGS HISTORICAL SOCIETY COLLECTION

plane of that era, had left all of its improvements when the facility was closed.

Celebrities began to build houses in the area. Lily Pons and Jolie Gabor and her beautiful daughters built their homes on the same hill. Kirk Douglas moved into the Las Palmas area, and Frank Sinatra built a large house on Alejo Road. Bob Hope, a long-time resident, was appointed Honorary Mayor.

Palm Springs' appellation as "Golf Capital of the World" included Thunderbird and Tamarisk Country Clubs as part of the city. Even Floyd Odlum's course in Indio was included in the count. Many of the day's tournaments were played on those courses.

Polo, popular before the war, was revived, and several indoor tournaments were played at the Field Club. Tennis tournaments at the Racquet Club and Tennis Club brought the city worldwide acclaim.

World-famous celebrities brought glamour and excitement to the desert. It is alleged that even United States Presidents Herbert Hoover and Franklin D. Roosevelt spent time here before the war. But, nothing equaled the furor of Dwight D. Eisenhower's arrival in February 1954. Over two thousand people were on hand to greet Ike and his wife Mamie.

The President arrived at 9:30 p.m. to be met by Governor Goodwin Knight, Paul Helms, Paul Hoffman and Mayor Florian Boyd. Crowds lined the streets as the presidential procession proceeded to Smoke Tree Ranch. Paul Helms' house became the Western White House. By 8:00 a.m. the next morning, President Eisenhower, Ben Hogan, Paul Helms and Paul Hoffman teed off at Tamarisk Country Club. The next day, at Thunderbird Country Club, he was joined by Hawthorne Dent, Paul Helms, Leonard Firestone and John Dawson.

The Spa Hotel, designed by architect William F. Cody, opened in April 1963 and was built to include the hot springs originally used by the Agua Caliente Band of Cahuilla Indians. While not the original developers of the resort, the tribe now owns and operates the facility which includes a casino.

PALM SPRINGS HISTORICAL SOCIETY COLLECTION

Mayor Bogert greets President John F. Kennedy on his first trip to Palm Springs in 1962. President Kennedy had spent a considerable amount of time at the Racquet Club during his terms as senator; this was his first visit as President.

PHOTO BY GEORGE AQUINO

During his visit, the El Mirador Hotel housed all the press and security people. The whole village turned out to entertain the press and anyone else connected with the presidential party. The seven days of President Eisenhower's visit brought more world recognition to Palm Springs than it had ever received before.

On the President's return to Washington, D.C., he signed the Equalization Bill, which finalized the Agua Caliente Indians' land allotments. Eisenhower made many return visits to Palm Springs and eventually retired to his home on the grounds of the Eldorado Country Club in 1961.

President Harry S. Truman also spent considerable time in the desert during this period, staying at the home of Phil Regan on Tamarisk Road.

By December 9, 1962, when President John F. Kennedy came to town on the first of several trips, villagers considered themselves experienced presidential hosts. Again, thousands of people turned out to catch a glimpse of this very popular president.

On February 20, 1964, Palm Springs was the scene of a major international event. President Lyndon Johnson had chosen the city for a meeting with Mexico's President Adolfo Lopez Mateos to resolve a long-standing dispute over a piece of land in Texas called the Chamizal.

The entourage consisted of the President, his wife Lady Bird, Secretary of State Dean Rusk and his wife and a contingent from the State Department. Lopez Mateos had a similar retinue from Mexico. The airport and the entire city were decorated with the flags of both countries. On hand to greet the presidents were two hundred white-costumed Mexicali residents.

On a trip to London in 1966, Mayor Bogert and Tony Owen induced Prince Philip to come to Palm Springs for a polo match. The Pathfinders, a local charity, were to share the proceeds of the match with Prince Philip's charity, "The Duke of Edinburgh Award for Young People."

Prince Philip *(right)* came to Palm Springs in 1966 to raise funds for the Duke of Edinburgh Award, a foundation for teenagers. He stayed at the home of Louis Taubman, played polo at Eldorado Country Club and was entertained by villagers. Meeting him at the airport are actress Donna Reed and Frank Bogert.
PHOTO BY PAUL POSPESIL

A crowd of several thousand attended the match between a Mexican team and a California team at Eldorado Polo Club. Montie Montana brought Prince Philip to the match in his four-up stagecoach and let him drive around the field so that everyone could see him.

The Louis Taubmans, who had loaned their home for President Johnson's visit, hosted Prince Philip and his entourage. A luncheon at their house was attended by four hundred of Southern California's most socially prominent people. Over one hundred reporters and photographers waited outside; only one photographer, Nancy Holmes, was permitted to take photos, pictures which she shared with all of the media.

President Gerald Ford had visited Palm Springs during his term as vice president. When his term of office as president expired in 1978, he returned to build a home next to Ambassador Leonard Firestone's house at Thunderbird Country Club. The Fords have been very active in all valley events, appearing at groundbreakings, hotel openings and charitable balls. The President has played in all major golf tournaments. Mrs. Ford brings considerable recognition to the valley through her alcohol and drug treatment center in Rancho Mirage.

Walter Annenberg, former Ambassador to the Court of St. James, and his wife Leonore, former Secretary of Protocol for President Reagan, built their beautiful estate in Rancho Mirage. Over the years, the famous guests they entertained would fill a book. For many years, President and Mrs. Ronald Reagan spent the New Year's week at Sunnylands, as the Annenbergs call their estate.

On February 27, 1983, Queen Elizabeth and Prince Philip arrived to visit the Annenbergs for several days; the following year Prince Charles paid a visit. The Annenbergs, like the Fords, have been very involved in valley life. The Palm Springs Desert Museum, Eisenhower Medical Center, Bob Hope Cultural Center and United Way are but a few of the recipients of their charity. They have been honored by many organizations for their contributions to the valley's culture.

The people who made Palm Springs world-famous, such as Albert Einstein, Samuel Untermyer, Mayor Jimmy Walker and Jimmy Swinnerton, would hardly be noticed today in the valley. On any given day during the winter season, over one hundred nationally known figures can be seen around the desert. On the Forbes 400 list of the country's most wealthy people, dozens have homes in the valley. They will not, however, be seen walking down Palm Canyon Drive as

Leonore and Walter Annenberg have hosted many dignitaries at their estate in Rancho Mirage and have been benefactors to many charities and cultural organizations in the valley.

PHOTO BY TOM BREWSTER, COURTESY PALM SPRINGS LIFE MAGAZINE

George Alexander and his son Bob built hundreds of homes in tracts all over Palm Springs. The home pictured was designed by architect William Krisel and built in 1959 in the Royal Desert Palms tract, now known as Twin Palms. The characteristic design elements of these homes are dramatic roof forms, high ceilings and clerestory windows capturing mountain views.
PHOTO BY JULIUS SHULMAN

frequently as they were seen in Palm Springs' early days.

The biggest growth in the history of Palm Springs began in the early 1960s when Jack Meiselman built the first large tract of reasonably-priced homes. Later, George Alexander and his son Bob built hundreds of homes in tracts all over the village. Sales were rapid; most tracts were sold out long before they were completed.

Dick Weiss and his father Jack came to town in 1962 with some fresh ideas which completely revolutionized the second-home concept. Sy Simon had built a cooperative project, but nobody had perfected the idea of condominiums until the Weiss family arrived. A new ordinance had to be written and many state laws modified before the idea was accepted. Today, over twelve thousand condos in Palm Springs and eighty-five percent of all second homes in the valley fit into this category.

During the 1970s, an attitude of no-growth spread throughout the city. The Planning Commission, City Council and most of the city's leaders were looking for ways to slow down development. A group of homeowners entitled "The Desert People United" exerted a strong influence, and the council eventually declared a six-month building moratorium.

The council came up with a new general plan which down-zoned several city areas, increasing animosity between the Agua Caliente Indians and the city as to the city's right to control Indian land.

In October 1977, the Under-Secretary of the Interior sent a memorandum to the city which stated that the city could not regulate zoning on Indian land. Mayor Russ Beirich and the City Council faced a tremendous problem, which was finally resolved by an agreement between the city and the tribe in which several parcels were restored to their former, less-restrictive zoning. The city was authorized to handle all zoning cases; however, if a controversy arose, the city could be overruled by the Agua Caliente Tribal Council.

Mayor Beirich and his council had barely resolved this problem when an even bigger one arose. On June 6, 1978, the state's voters passed Proposition 13. The city, consequently, was faced with a $3,300,000 tax loss. By June 17, the new budget had cut sixty-five positions, closed two branch libraries and made major cuts in every department.

By the 1980s, an entirely new philosophy toward development was in evidence. The council elected in 1982 began an aggressive program. The Redevelopment Agency, which had been in operation for years, was activated and seven districts were put into position. The downtown area was the first priority. Within the first year, the Desert Fashion Plaza and Maxim's Hotel were on the drawing board.

The agency condemned the entire block from Andreas Road to Amado Road and Palm Canyon Drive to Belardo Road. Andreas Road was vacated to make room for Saks Fifth Avenue, and the building which had been the Bunker Garage and Village Pharmacy was demolished. Other buildings razed included the Village Theater, the Chi Chi, Palm Springs Hotel and Nate's Delicatessen.

The beautiful Desert Fashion Plaza and Maxim's opened in 1986 with 1,400 underground parking spaces and a number of quality shops. *[Eds. Note: As of 2002, Maxim's has become the Hyatt Regency Suites and the Desert Fashion Plaza's future is unknown.]* The Marquis Hotel in Section 14 and the Shilo Hotel on North Palm Canyon Drive opened shortly afterwards.

An agreement was made with Texas developer Trammell Crow to build the four hundred-room Wyndham Hotel, which opened in November 1987, and an adjoining convention center on Avenida Caballeros and Tahquitz Canyon Way, which opened in February 1988.

The ground-breaking ceremony for the new Wyndham Hotel and the Convention Center was held on April 25, 1986. Former President Gerald Ford, Mayor Frank Bogert and Trammell Crow from Dallas, Texas, were on hand to start construction. Trammell Crow, owner of the Wyndham Hotel chain, is one of the largest developers in the country with many shopping centers, multistory buildings and prestigious hotels to his credit.

PHOTO COURTESY OF THE DESERT SUN

The famous oval pool at the Palm Springs Tennis Club, opened in 1938, was a well known gathering place for visitors and a favorite of photographers.
PALM SPRINGS HISTORICAL SOCIETY COLLECTION

Palm Canyon Drive in 1934 looked extremely bare without its palm trees. The planting began in 1947. This photo was taken looking south from the 200 block of North Palm Canyon Drive.

PALM SPRINGS HISTORICAL SOCIETY COLLECTION

It was often said in the 1940s that you could shoot a cannon down Palm Canyon Drive anytime in the summer and not hit a soul. This photo, shot in August 1946 in the center of town, shows three moving automobiles and five parked vehicles.

RAY JONES COLLECTION

RIGHT: Pretty Louise Bramlett was chosen queen of Palm Springs' first Desert Circus in 1934. Louise was the daughter of Mrs. George Roberson. Her stepfather was the son of The Desert Inn's owner, Nellie Coffman.

PALM SPRINGS HISTORICAL SOCIETY COLLECTION

BELOW: Nellie Coffman joins architect Harry J. Williams in the ribbon-cutting ceremony in 1936 for the new Palm Springs Plaza. Williams, a very successful Dayton, Ohio, architect, was brought to the desert by Mrs. Julia S. Carnell and never returned to the east. His two architect sons, Stewart and Roger, remained here with their children and grandchildren.

PALM SPRINGS HISTORICAL SOCIETY COLLECTION

ABOVE AND INSET, RIGHT: Warren Pinney, manager of the El Mirador Hotel, and his publicity man were always looking for something new to contribute to the newsreels of the Sunday swimming and diving show. The photo above from 1936 shows performers *(from the top)* Bill Lewin, Mickey Riley, Dutch Smith and Farid Samaica doing water acrobatics. Inset photo, (c. 1937) shows the author, publicity man for the El Mirador at the time, as the first rider of the bucking horse, fully clothed, over the pool.

FRANK BOGERT COLLECTION

RIGHT: Jackie Cooper, a famous child star and successful director, gives actress Bonita Granville an underwater kiss in the El Mirador Hotel pool. Jackie was a Palm Springs resident for many years, as were Bonita and her husband Jack Wrather. The Wrathers owned the L'Horizon Hotel in Palm Springs for over twenty years.

PHOTO BY FRANK BOGERT

LEFT: Hollywood starlet Frances Neel and a newborn colt are photographed at Rogers Stables in 1939. Neel later married actor Van Heflin.

PHOTO BY FRANK BOGERT

BELOW: Dick Whittington, who took the photo of the author on a horse (shown on page 2 of this book), was considered one of the best photographers in the country. Warren Pinney hired him to take pictures for a new El Mirador Hotel brochure. Here two models are shown picking desert primroses in April 1935.

PHOTO BY DICK WHITTINGTON

ABOVE: Dorothy Lamour and Robert Preston, two of the most popular Hollywood stars in 1936, walk in the gardens of the El Mirador Hotel.

PHOTO BY FRANK BOGERT

LEFT: During part of the 1920s, 1930s and 1940s, a little man with a magnifying glass sat under a paloverde tree reading people's palms. This village character was John Hastie, who in the days of silent movies played "The Mysterious Rider." Celebrities, visitors and townspeople alike declared that his predictions had an uncanny way of coming true. For twenty-five years Hastie sat on his throne, a cement-based tree on Baristo Road just off Palm Canyon Drive.

PHOTO BY GAIL THOMPSON

RIGHT: For over a decade, Priscilla Chaffey edited the local weekly paper. Everyone read the *The Limelight,* as it contained all the local news. Priscilla was never seen without her concho belt and most of the time wore a Indian buckskin skirt to work. Her husband John, seen here with her at the Polo Club in 1939, was a prominent Realtor.

PHOTO BY FRANK BOGERT

BELOW: Robert Ransom was a leading Palm Springs Realtor for many years and was instrumental in the development of the Plaza and the Carnell Building.

PHOTO BY FRANK BOGERT

ABOVE: Leslie Charteris and his wife at the Doll House in 1938. Leslie was the author of *The Saint,* a collection of mystery stories that were later made into a popular television series. His English accent, monocle and oriental features made a strange combination with his constant cowboy hat and western attire. The Charteris' owned a house at the Racquet Club Estates, and he showed up daily at the club in Levis and plaid shirts.

PHOTO BY FRANK BOGERT

BELOW: Among the large estate houses of the 1920s was one built by Alvah Hicks for Carrie Birge. Shortly after Carrie left for Paris, her son Humphrey *(below),* and his wife Ethel took over the estate. The Birges' daughter Caroline, who had married Alvah's son Harold, has been active locally for many years, as has her son, Jim Hicks, who has served on many city boards and commissions. Young Hicks was president of Eadie Adams Real Estate, one of Palm Springs' largest and most successful real estate offices. The Birge estate was purchased in 1935 by Ruth Hardy, who developed it into a quality hotel. It continues today under the ownership of Mel Haber, who has maintained its reputation as one of Palm Springs' finest.

PHOTO COURTESY CAROLINE BIRGE SUMMERS

When the Palm Springs Rotary Club began in February 1941, it was discovered that Paul Harris, the national founder, lived in the city. George Relf, the first local president, accepts the charter as Art Bailey, seated, looks on.

PHOTO BY FRANK BOGERT

RIGHT: The Vaqueros del Desierto's first ride in 1938 was a huge success. This photo was taken as riders returned to Palm Springs at the end of the five-day trek. *Left to right:* John Cooper, Newt House, Jackie Cooper, Cliff Meade, Frank Bogert, Bob Mount, Bob Ransom and Harvey Ellis.

PHOTO BY JOHN MILLER

BELOW: El Mirador guests are off on a breakfast ride in Trav Rogers' old Brewster Road Coach. The coach stood in the front yard of Chuck Coffman's house for many years. Chuck was Nellie Coffman's grandson.

PHOTO BY FRANK BOGERT

RIGHT: A group of local horsemen organized a trail ride in 1938 patterned after the Rancheros Visitadores. Frank Bennett, Earl Coffman, Warren Pinney, Trav Rogers and Frank Bogert, planners of the event, named it Vaqueros del Desierto. The first ride was up Morongo Canyon to Yucca Valley, Warren Wells and Keys Ranch, now in the Joshua Tree National Park. The return route to Palm Springs was a long desert ride down Thousand Palms Canyon. The ride took place every year until the outbreak of the war in 1941. Sam Buckingham was the group's first president; Cliff Meade from Pasadena became president when the group re-formed after the war. Still going strong, the ride now takes place in a different area of Southern California every year.

PALM SPRINGS HISTORICAL SOCIETY COLLECTION

Earl Coffman in 1938 when he was manager of The Desert Inn. Photo taken on the first Vaqueros del Desierto ride. He was one of the founders of the Vaqueros and an ardent horseman, who also helped organize the Desert Riders in 1930.

PHOTO BY FRANK BOGERT

Young stars Bonita Granville and Jackie Cooper take a dinner ride in 1940. Bonita later married Jack Wrather, and they were the owners of several hotel properties including L'Horizon in Palm Springs.

PHOTO BY FRANK BOGERT

ABOVE: Robert Taylor, a good horseman, spent a great deal of time riding in the desert. He took part in the first Vaqueros del Desierto ride in 1938 and kept his horses at Trav Rogers' stable during the winter.

PHOTO BY GAIL THOMPSON

BELOW: Harold Hicks on the Vaqueros del Desierto ride in 1938. Following his father Alvah's footsteps, he improved the water system that was eventually worth six million dollars by the time he sold it to the Palm Springs Water Company. Hicks also ran a successful real estate office and was active in civic affairs. Harold and his wife Caroline had four children: Gail, Jim, Jean and Dennis.

PHOTO BY FRANK BOGERT

Trav Rogers leads a group of ladies on a pack trip up Palm Canyon in 1939.

PHOTO BY FRANK BOGERT

ABOVE: Arthur Lake, known for his role as Dagwood Bumstead in films and later radio, his wife Patricia and aunt, Miss Ethel Davies, sister of Marion Davies, enjoy a buckboard ride while vacationing in Palm Springs. This 1939 photo was taken at the zenith of Arthur's career. He later made the desert his home, living in the area until his death in 1986.

PHOTO BY FRANK BOGERT.

LEFT: Pat Dougherty and Pete Young look over Earl Coffman's shoulder at the war news in 1940 during a Vaqueros ride.

PHOTO BY FRANK BOGERT

The Mexican Colony was very active in the town's early days. Its annual fiesta was always a big community event. Pictured are Ruth Roberson, granddaughter of Nellie Coffman, holding little Olivia Avila. *Standing, left to right:* Mercedes Rios, princesses Vickie Ortega, Hortensia Ortega, Helen Prieto, Lecha Mediano, Candy Reyes, Rafaela Marmolejo, Helen Ayala and Lupe Rios. *Upper left:* Manuel Marmolejo and Frank Bogert, standing next to Emily Herrera. The man and young boy in front are unidentified, c. 1945.

VIRGINIA MARMOLEJO COLLECTION

RIGHT: John J. Raskob was an industrial giant from New York. A director of DuPont and General Motors, he also financed and served as the Chairman of the Board of the Empire State Building. After spending three seasons as a guest at the El Mirador, he bought 2,500 acres in Desert Hot Springs in 1938. He planned to build a complete city, but abandoned the project after the re-election of President Roosevelt. A popular resident, John escorted many of the local girls on social occasions. After the war, Ray Ryan bought the land from Raskob's estate. Today, it is the site of the finest residences in Desert Hot Springs, including the Mission Lakes Country Club. Raskob is shown in this 1939 photograph with musician Bill Slivers on a breakfast ride.

PHOTO BY FRANK BOGERT

BELOW: Film star Connie Talmadge, western movie star and noted rodeo performer Montie Montana, and Frank Bogert in 1934. Freeman Gosden shot the picture of the trio on a breakfast ride.

FRANK BOGERT COLLECTION

ABOVE: Jack Krindler *(right)* standing with an unknown party-goer. Charlie Berns and Jack Krindler owned Jack and Charlie's Club in New York. They joined the "horsey set" of the village, stayed at the B-BAR-H Ranch in Desert Hot Springs, and were seen daily at Trav Rogers' Mink and Manure Club. Jack became an avid rider and bought chaps, hats and jackets from local cowboys. One of the Desert Riders' best trails is named the Berns Trail.

PHOTO BY FRANK BOGERT

LEFT: By accident, Charlie Farrell and Janet Gaynor both showed up in white clown suits for a Big Top Ball at the Racquet Club. Janet was married to famous designer, Adrian, at the time. Charlie had been married for several years to Virginia Valli.

PHOTO BY FRANK BOGERT

RIGHT: Charles Farrell was at the top of his acting career in 1927 after the release of the famous silent film *Seventh Heaven*, co-starring Janet Gaynor. Exhausted from making films, he came to Palm Springs in 1931, and a year later formed a partnership with his friend, actor Ralph Bellamy. They purchased fifty-three acres of land for thirty-five hundred dollars and built the world-famous Racquet Club. Charlie became very active in village affairs; in 1948, he was elected to the city council and served as mayor for five years. The Racquet Club was a haven for movie stars, and Charlie, as mayor, brought considerable fame to the small, though growing, town of Palm Springs.

PALM SPRINGS
HISTORICAL SOCIETY COLLECTION

Charlie Farrell and Janet Gaynor attend an event at the Racquet Club some forty years after their picture *Seventh Heaven*.

PALM SPRINGS
DESERT MUSEUM COLLECTION

RIGHT: Jimmie, Trav Rogers' daughter, was a beautiful girl who became famous around the horse show circuit. She was Rodeo Queen, Desert Circus Queen and an all-around champion in the state horse show. Here, she is seen modeling his and hers sports jackets with Charlie Farrell at the Racquet Club. She later married Milton Hicks, owner of the Palm Springs Builders' Supply.

PHOTO BY FRANK BOGERT

LEFT: Jane Wyman and Charlie Farrell help René, the Racquet Club chef, prepare the turkey for Thanksgiving in 1938.

PHOTO BY FRANK BOGERT

BELOW: Virginia Valli was a big star long before Charlie Farrell, her husband, became famous. When Charlie bought out partner Ralph Bellamy, Virginia helped him operate the Racquet Club. While Charlie was in the Navy for three years during World War II, she ran it by herself. The handsome couple is shown in 1939.

PHOTO BY FRANK BOGERT

BELOW: One of Charlie Farrell's favorite photos was this pose with his three polo ponies.

PALM SPRINGS HISTORICAL SOCIETY COLLECTION

Lunch around the Racquet Club pool was a daily sellout. Reservations for tables were a must, especially on days when a fashion show was staged.

PALM SPRINGS HISTORICAL SOCIETY COLLECTION

LEFT: Rudy Vallee goes over his program for a show at the Racquet Club with owners Ralph Bellamy and Charlie Farrell. Club tennis pro, Les Stoefen, looks on, c. 1939.

PHOTO BY FRANK BOGERT

Bing Crosby was a frequent Racquet Club visitor. Here, he toasts the New Year of 1940. In 1951, he built one of the first homes at Thunderbird.
PHOTO BY FRANK BOGERT

RIGHT: Jobina Ralston and husband Richard Arlen were among the many stars from the movie colony who frequented the Racquet Club in the 1930s.
PHOTO BY FRANK BOGERT

ABOVE: Paul Lukas *(left)* was at the peak of his forty-year career as an actor in 1938. A founding member of the Racquet Club and an avid tennis player, Lukas is shown here with Ruth Stoefen, wife of pro Les Stoefen, and Reggie Owen, popular character actor in the 1930s.
PHOTO BY FRANK BOGERT

BELOW: Joe Schenck, famous Hollywood producer, dances a jitterbug with Ruth Selwyn, a local resident, at the Racquet Club in 1938.
PHOTO BY FRANK BOGERT

ABOVE: Popular band leader Artie Shaw is photographed at the Racquet Club on his honeymoon with Lana Turner in 1939.

PHOTO BY FRANK BOGERT

ABOVE: Joe Schenck, *second from left,* MGM producer, owned a home in Palm Springs for many years. He's shown here at the Farrell's house with Ruth and Lester Stoefen, Ruth Warburton and Katherine Bellamy in 1938.

PALM SPRINGS HISTORICAL SOCIETY COLLECTION

ABOVE: Marlene Dietrich and Leslie Howard join the festivities at the Racquet Club. Marlene had a home in Palm Springs and her daughter was a student at the high school.

PHOTO BY FRANK BOGERT

LEFT: Few people knew Pop Farrell, Charlie Farrell's father, who ran the back of the house at the Racquet Club. He had the keys to food and liquor storerooms and issued all items to the bartenders and chefs. At the time this photo was taken, he was 84 years old and had just married a young lady.

PALM SPRINGS HISTORICAL SOCIETY COLLECTION

RIGHT: Three of Hollywood's movie greats, Don Ameche, Robert Taylor and Charles Farrell, are photographed in 1939 at the entrance to the Racquet Club.

PHOTO BY FRANK BOGERT

BELOW: A rare photograph captures the three Ritz Brothers together. Arlene Judge, a well-known star of that era, is at left; Mrs. Harry Ritz is the other lady in the picture. The photo was taken in 1938 at the Racquet Club.

PHOTO BY FRANK BOGERT

ABOVE: Crooner Rudy Vallee brought his band to Palm Springs in 1939 to broadcast his radio show from the Racquet Club. Pictured are club owners Ralph Bellamy and Charlie Farrell with Rudy. The trio is admiring a cake sent by Al Wertheimer, owner of the Dunes Club in Cathedral City, to wish them success.

PALM SPRINGS HISTORICAL SOCIETY COLLECTION

RIGHT: Dave Butler, a top movie director, gets into the spirit of the Desert Circus as he directs *Two Guys From Texas*, which was filmed at Thunderbird Ranch in 1947. Butler had worked with Charlie Farrell in *Seventh Heaven*.

PHOTO BY FRANK BOGERT

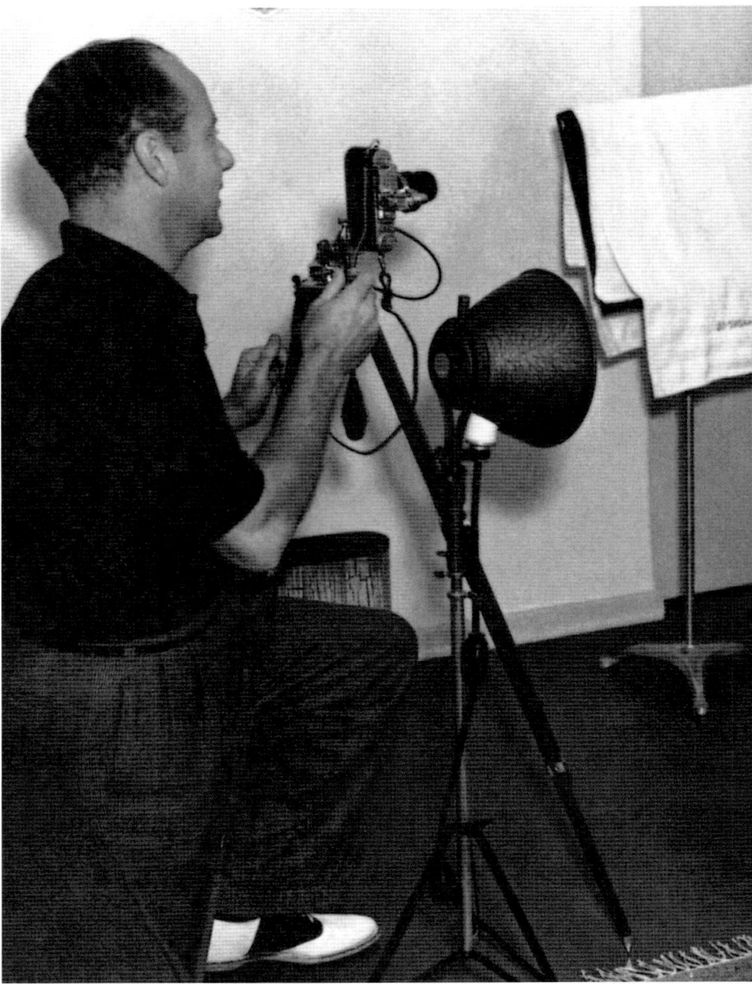

ABOVE: Ray Ryan, wealthy oilman and owner of the El Mirador Hotel, hams it up with "Banjo Eyes" Eddie Cantor. Cantor's house was behind the El Mirador. Every day he walked to the hotel to have breakfast with Ryan.

PHOTO BY FRANK BOGERT

ABOVE CENTER: Freeman Gosden and Charles Correll, of the radio comedy team of *Amos and Andy*, broadcast from the El Mirador tower nightly in the 1930s. Gosden, an avid photographer, used the tower as his studio in the daytime.

PHOTO BY FRANK BOGERT

RIGHT: *Amos and Andy* was by far the most popular 1930s radio program. For many winters, the show was broadcast from the El Mirador's tower. Seen here at the pool about 1933 are Freeman Gosden (Amos), Madaline Lee (Miss Blue), and Charlie Correll (Andy). Freeman and Charlie wrote all of their material and performed all the men's voices. They hired Madaline to handle all of the female roles.

PHOTO BY TONY BURKE

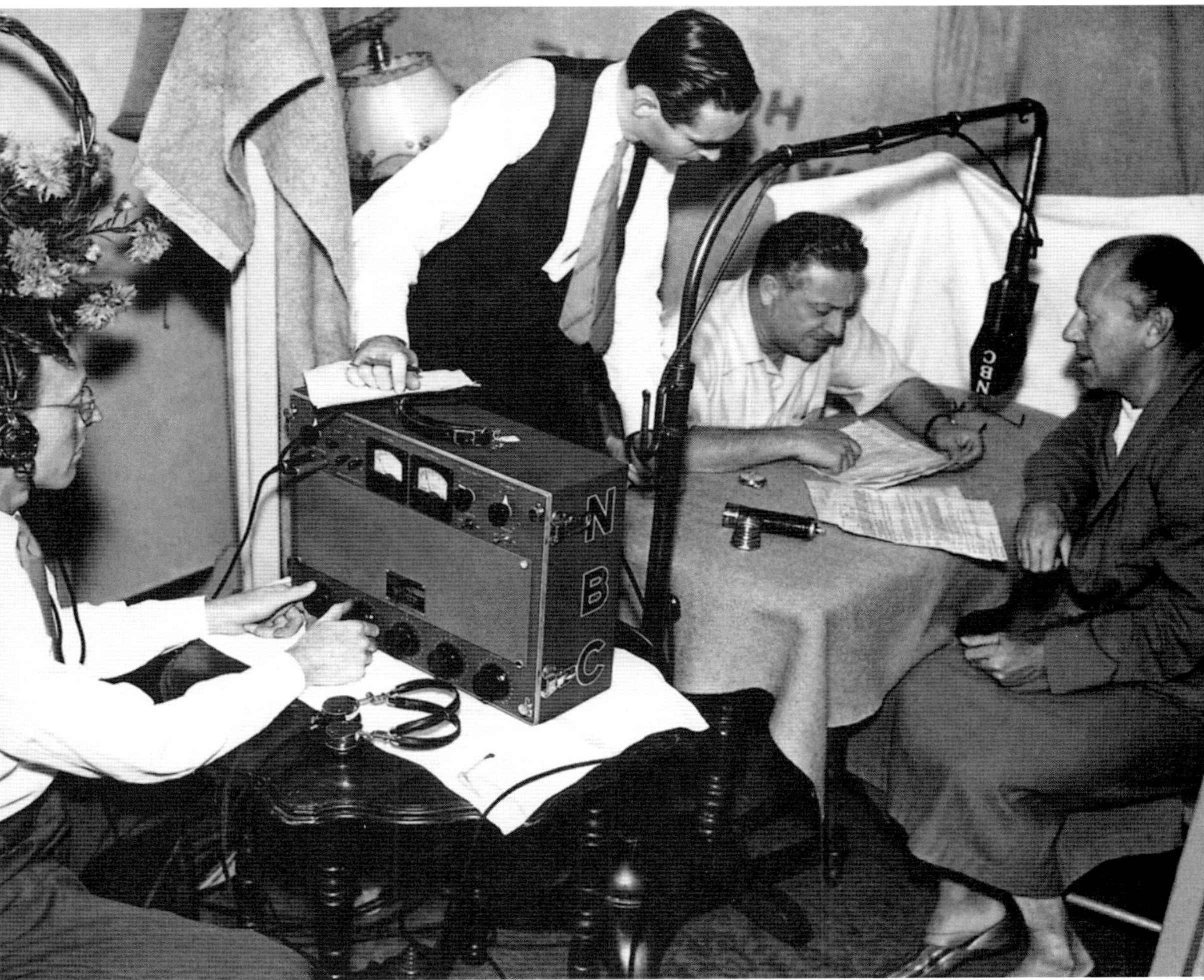

ABOVE: For six years prior to World War II, Amos (Freeman Gosden) and Andy (Charlie Correll) broadcast from the El Mirador Hotel. During the day they wrote the script and at 7:00 p.m. they performed the show. For many years, the Gosdens and the Corrells had homes in the desert. Summers, they returned to Chicago to broadcast. When Gosden retired, he moved to Eldorado Country Club and was a constant companion of Dwight Eisenhower.

FRANK BOGERT COLLECTION

LEFT: Shown seated at his piano is Hoagy Carmichael, perhaps best known for his composition *Stardust*. Hoagy was one of Thunderbird's first residents.

PHOTO BY FRANK BOGERT

RIGHT: Shirley Temple was a frequent Desert Inn guest. In this photo of her as a teenager, taken at the beginning of World War II, she helps two GIs position a sign for a USO fundraiser.

PHOTO BY FRANK BOGERT

BELOW: Since meat was rationed during the war, it was a red letter day when a shipment arrived in the village. Hutch Mosely and Joe Butler take care of a crowd of eager patrons at the local Safeway market on North Palm Canyon Drive.

PALM SPRINGS HISTORICAL SOCIETY COLLECTION

ABOVE: A 1942 aerial view of Smoke Tree Stables on East Palm Canyon Drive, now the location of the Smoke Tree Shopping Center. Earl Proebstell, the original operator of the stables, sold them to Rod Abbott in 1932. Later owners included Tex Miller and Ken Johnson. Ken's son Rod now operates the stables, the last public riding stable in Palm Springs in its new location south of Smoke Tree Ranch.

PHOTO BY GAIL THOMPSON

BELOW: Palm Desert in 1945 was a barren alluvial fan through which passed the Palms to Pines Highway. Located on Highway 111, there were only a couple of small buildings and entrance roads to date groves. The area was known as Palm Village for many years. The clear area on the left of the photo was the location for Patton's tank repair depot during World War II. The dark line is Whitewater Wash.

PHOTO COURTESY RAY JONES

ABOVE: In 1940, the United States Army Corps of Engineers began construction of a large landing site on Section 18 of tribal land. (This parcel was purchased by the city from the Indians after the war.) They also used the eastern half of Pearl McManus' land on Section 13 to build hangars, soldiers' quarters and an officers' club. In this photo, the old runway on Section 14 can be seen at top right. To the left is the Field Club with a polo field and a half-mile track at the corner of Ramon Road and Sunrise Way. This land is now the site of Palm Springs Stadium, the Palm Springs Public Library and Sunrise Plaza. Pearl McManus gave a right of way for the road in the center and insisted it be called McCallum Way in honor of her father.

FRANK MOORE COLLECTION

RIGHT: The U.S. Ferry Command tower in this photo sits on the exact site of the present fountain which was donated to the city by Pearl McManus. The buildings on the right were used after the war as offices for the airport. Beyond them is the site of the present city hall.

PHOTO BY JOHNNY PAGORIA

ABOVE: During the war, the El Mirador Hotel's thirty-acre property became part of the Torney General Hospital, a sprawling complex that totalled more than one hundred acres. The land in the center of the picture is now Ruth Hardy Park. After the war the barracks were sold and individually moved to locations all over the desert.

PHOTO COURTESY RAY JONES

LEFT: Lucille Ball was a budding starlet when this photo was taken at the El Mirador Hotel in 1938. She spent many seasons in Palm Springs and built one of the first houses at Thunderbird Country Club.

PHOTO BY JOHN MILLER

BELOW: For many years, gambling clubs flourished in the little town of Cathedral City. Al Wertheimer ran the Dunes and Frank Portnoy managed the Cove. Earl Sausser's 139 Club was the most popular. He later sold it to Walter Melrose, a successful attorney and large property owner in Cathedral City. Melrose and his wife Cleo are shown dining at the Chi Chi in Palm Springs.

PHOTO BY BILL RASHALL, PEG STANS RASHALL COLLECTION

LEFT: Jack Benny and his wife Mary Livingstone were long-time residents of Palm Springs. For many years, his radio show was broadcast from the Plaza Theater, bringing much fame and glamour to the village. Benny is snapped here as he gives guest star Bing Crosby a cookie to loosen his vocal cords.

PALM SPRINGS HISTORICAL SOCIETY COLLECTION

RIGHT: Famous opera singer Lily Pons spent several seasons as a guest at Ruth Hardy's Ingleside Inn before she built her house in Palm Springs. When the American flag was flying over her residence, you always knew she was in town.

PALM SPRINGS HISTORICAL SOCIETY COLLECTION

BELOW: At a typical Racquet Club party stand William Powell, Charlie Farrell and local realtor Harold Hicks, flanked by Georgina Poston and an unidentified man. Seated are Mousie Powell, Virginia Farrell and Mr. and Mrs. Sherman Hull.

FRANK BOGERT COLLECTION

BELOW: Margaret O'Brien was a popular child star in the 1940s. A frequent winter guest, she poses on the diving board at the Ingleside Inn.

PALM SPRINGS HISTORICAL SOCIETY COLLECTION

The 1939 queen of the Desert Circus was Janice Bibo, whose mother, Ruth Bibo, was an early pioneer and the owner of the Acoma Indian Curio Shop. Janice later married Frank Bogert, and their three daughters Cindy Lamm, Donna Higueras and Denni Russell still live in Palm Springs.

PHOTO BY FRANK BOGERT

BELOW: Paulette Goddard, a winter guest in Palm Springs for many years, was chosen to lead the parade as Desert Circus Queen in 1940.

PALM SPRINGS HISTORICAL SOCIETY COLLECTION

ABOVE: Stan Rosin and his wife Hermine in the 1939 Desert Circus Parade. Stanley owned the El Encanto Hotel at the time and became one of the owners of La Plaza. An ardent golfer at Tamarisk, he is one of the very few who could "shoot his age."

PHOTO BY FRANK BOGERT

RIGHT: Ethel V. Mars, owner of the Mars Candy Company, gets put into stocks at the Kangaroo Court for wearing a funny hat during Desert Circus Week in 1939.

PHOTO BY FRANK BOGERT

ABOVE: Tom Mix, a legendary cowboy screen star, is shown at the Field Club during the Desert Circus in 1937.

PHOTO BY JOHN MILLER

ABOVE: Robert Wagner and Ray Ryan with Joan Whitney, prepare to lead the 1956 circus parade. The red-jacketed horsemen behind were from the famous Los Angeles Sheriffs Mounted Posse.

PHOTO BY FRANK BOGERT

RIGHT: Jane Withers, a child star whose popularity was second only to Shirley Temple's, was a frequent desert visitor. She is shown here at the Kangaroo Court during Desert Circus week with a 7'6" giant from Hollywood. Bill Reichel, Rancho Mirage farmer, and Hal Kelley look on.

PHOTO BY FRANK BOGERT

ABOVE: The Palm Springs Women's Club celebrates its two-year anniversary with a float in the 1940 Desert Circus Parade. Bullock's store at The Desert Inn is in the background.

PHOTO BY FRANK BOGERT

BELOW: Charlie McCarthy and Edgar Bergen in the 1947 Desert Circus Parade. The Village Theater and the Chi Chi gave way to the Desert Fashion Plaza.

PHOTO BY GAIL THOMPSON

ABOVE: Skinny Ennis, a famous bandleader is shown here with wife Carmine at the Desert Circus' Kangaroo Court in 1940.

PHOTO BY FRANK BOGERT

The 1956 Desert Circus Ball at the El Mirador was a spectacular costumed event, featuring Metropolitan Opera star and local resident Lily Pons as queen and Ray Ryan as king. Ryan, millionaire oilman from Indiana, owned the El Mirador Hotel. "Nubian" slaves with ostrich feather fans cooled the royal couple and eight princesses.

PHOTO BY FRANK BOGERT

Chuck Connors as Grand Marshal of a Desert Circus Parade. Connors, a well-known actor, was a resident at the Canyon Country Club for many years. This photo caught him riding past a famous local landmark, Don the Beachcomber, at the corner of Via Lola and North Palm Canyon Drive.

PHOTO BY PAUL POSPESIL

ABOVE: One entry in the Desert Circus Parade of 1949 was the Desert Museum float featuring Lex Barker, the Tarzan of this period.

PALM SPRINGS DESERT MUSEUM COLLECTION

BELOW LEFT: Gene Autry was Grand Marshal of the Mounted Police Rodeo Parade in 1958. With him are Sue Ane Langdon, a Hollywood starlet, and Robert White, Chief of Police.

PALM SPRINGS HISTORICAL SOCIETY COLLECTION

ABOVE: Grand Marshals for the 1948 Desert Circus Parade were Bob Hope and Jerry Colona, a regular on the *Bob Hope Show.*

PALM SPRINGS HISTORICAL SOCIETY COLLECTION

RIGHT: For many years, the Southern Pacific Railroad brought most of the winter guests to Palm Springs. Each hotel had a bus for transporting visitors from the station, located nine miles outside of town. The railroad also greatly helped to promote the city with posters and campaigns that brought tourists to the sun country.

PHOTO BY JOHN SHAW, JR.

BELOW: Southern Pacific Train No. 1, "The Sunset Limited," arrives at the Palm Springs Station on March 6, 1955.

PHOTO BY JOHN SHAW, JR.

ABOVE: In 1940, the Lang Airline Service connected Palm Springs and Los Angeles with daily flights in a twin Beechcraft. The airport was then located at Alejo Road and Avenida Caballeros.

PALM SPRINGS HISTORICAL SOCIETY COLLECTION

BELOW: Although American Airlines started regular service to Palm Springs in 1941, World War II brought it to an end. The inaugural service in a new DC-3, called Flagship Palm Springs, landed at the little airport in Section 14 and found a large crowd waiting to see what was, at that time, the largest plane in the sky.

PHOTO BY FRANK BOGERT

The entire Roberson family is photographed in 1948 on their return from a Hawaiian vacation. *Left to right:* Louise Schilling, Claude Valeur, Claude's wife Ruth, Docksie Schilling, and Alta and George Roberson. Louise Schilling, Mrs. Roberson's daughter, was queen of the first Desert Circus in 1934. Ruth Valeur was a successful interior decorator in Palm Springs.

PHOTO BY FRANK BOGERT

Jimmy Swinnerton, an acclaimed artist, and his wife were frequent visitors at The Desert Inn. *Left to right:* Gretchen Swinnerton, Nellie Coffman, Mrs. Clyde Forsythe (wife of a famous painter) and Jimmy Swinnerton.

PALM SPRINGS HISTORICAL SOCIETY COLLECTION

The Desert Inn in 1951 before it was demolished to erect the Desert Inn Fashion Plaza, a shopping mall. Tom O'Donnell's house on the hill is all that exists today of Nellie Coffman's holdings. Bungalows near the foot of the mountain are at the site of the Palm Springs Desert Museum.

PHOTO BY GAIL THOMPSON

LEFT: Frank Bogert and Lucille Ball at Thunderbird Country Club.
FRANK BOGERT COLLECTION

BELOW: John Morris, one of the city's most famous painters, greets glamorous Gloria Swanson at the El Mirador Hotel in 1952.
PHOTO BY CONRAD HUG

BELOW: Clark Gable and his wife Kay (the former Kay Spreckles) wait their turn to bowl at Palm Springs Lanes with Frank Bogert keeping score. The Gables built a home at the Bermuda Dunes Country Club.
PHOTO BY CONRAD HUG

ABOVE: Bing Crosby, who loved a casual style of dress, looks just right for the 1952 luau at Thunderbird Country Club.
PALM SPRINGS HISTORICAL SOCIETY COLLECTION

ABOVE: Actress Barbara Stanwyck dines with Los Angeles' famous sheriff, Gene Biscailuz, at the El Mirador Hotel while Frank Bogert looks on.

PHOTO BY CONRAD HUG

ABOVE: Local newsman Bill Rashall *(right)* interviews world-famous radio commentator Walter Winchell. Winchell's visit coincided with President Eisenhower's 1954 trip to Palm Springs.

PALM SPRINGS HISTORICAL SOCIETY COLLECTION

RIGHT: Movie star Donna Reed and her husband Tony Owen, producer of *The Donna Reed Show,* lived in Palm Springs for many years. In this 1954 photo, Donna was a cover girl for the El Mirador's brochure and the hotel menu.

PHOTO BY BILL ANDERSON

BELOW: Famous hotelier Conrad Hilton dances with a lady at the Racquet Club's New Year's Eve party, c. 1954.

PHOTO BY PAUL POSPESIL

Photo of the rodeo grounds in 1950 during the annual Mounted Police Rodeo. In 1961, the grounds were replaced by Angels Stadium, home of Gene Autry's California Angels.

PHOTO BY FRANK BOGERT

ABOVE: A western party at the El Mirador Hotel in 1952 attracted Rita Hayworth and Jack Wilson; Frank Bogert is in the background.

PHOTO BY CONRAD HUG

ABOVE: Joe Butler, manager of the Safeway store in Palm Springs, and Hollywood star Polly Bergen are photographed on a moonlight ride in 1966, the year Polly was the Queen of the Desert Circus Parade.

PHOTO BY PAUL POSPESIL

RIGHT: Walt Disney was a frequent visitor at Smoke Tree Ranch in Palm Springs.

FRANK BOGERT COLLECTION

LEFT: "Auntie" Pearl McManus rarely smiled for a picture. Mayor Ed McCoubrey, on a Desert Riders breakfast in 1959, must have told her a good joke just as the photo was taken.

PHOTO BY GAIL THOMPSON

BELOW: Frederick Loewe, whose works included such successful musicals as *Camelot*, *My Fair Lady* and *Paint Your Wagon*, lived in Palm Springs for years. His contributions to desert charities were phenomenal. In 1958, he led the Rodeo Parade, an honor bestowed on him by the Mounted Police.

PALM SPRINGS HISTORICAL SOCIETY COLLECTION

BELOW: Earl Cordrey was a nationally-known magazine illustrator and artist in Palm Springs. In 1961, he drew this sketch of Pearl McManus, *(above)* which captured her personality better than any photograph. Earl designed the city seal and taught painting for many years at the Palette Club.

PALM SPRINGS HISTORICAL SOCIETY COLLECTION

At the age of 65, Zaddie Bunker learned to fly, received her private pilot's license and bought her own plane, a Navion she called "Zaddie's Rockin' Chair II." She was famous across the country as the "flying grandmother." Besides being an excellent mechanic and pilot, she was still an avid horseback rider and often participated in morning rides.

PHOTO BY FRANK BOGERT

Four pioneer ladies lunching at the Tennis Club (c. 1951). *From left:* Ruth Bibo, who came to Palm Springs in 1930, owned the Acoma Indian Curio Shop, and became Frank Bogert's mother-in-law; Mary Grant, whose husband, Fred, built the first houses in Smoke Tree Ranch; Pearl McManus, daughter of John McCallum; and Zaddie Bunker, who started the Bunker Garage in 1917 and was the mother-in-law of Earle Strebe.

PHOTO BY VIC CULINA, PALM SPRINGS HISTORICAL SOCIETY COLLECTION

Three Palm Springs pioneers, *(left to right)* Henrietta Parker, who at the age 100 was Palm Springs' oldest living pioneer; Miss Katherine Finchy; and Jennie Leonesio. The lady at the far right is their friend Connie Contois. They are attending a party honoring Katherine Finchy. Henrietta Parker, Zaddie Bunker's younger sister, came to Palm Springs from Missouri in 1914. Jennie Leonesio, who arrived in 1918, was the mother of Bill Leonesio, Palm Springs' first fire chief.

PALM SPRINGS HISTORICAL SOCIETY COLLECTION

ABOVE: Former President Harry Truman, *(center)* visited Palm Springs in 1953. He joins hands with *(from left)* Charlie Farrell, Frank Bogert, Palm Springs Police Chief Gus Kettman and Phil Regan at Regan's Palm Springs estate, on the southeast corner of Via Miraleste and Tamarisk Road.

PALM SPRINGS HISTORICAL SOCIETY COLLECTION

LEFT: Ray Corliss, Palm Springs resident since 1951, bon vivant and raconteur, was co-chairman of the Desert Circus, a founder of the Palm Springs Club, and with Frank Bogert, founder of Cabalgatas Internationales.

RAY CORLISS COLLECTION

LEFT: Palm Springs City Council in 1954-1955. *Seated, left to right:* Ruth Hardy, Mayor Florian Boyd and Jerry Nathanson. *Standing:* Frank Miller, Jerry Sanborn, Earle Strebe and Ted McKinney.

PALM SPRINGS HISTORICAL SOCIETY COLLECTION

RIGHT: Three luminaries light up the 1963 Bob Hope Desert Golf Classic: Bob Hope, Frank Sinatra and Dean Martin.

PHOTO BY BILL RASHALL

BELOW: Frank Bogert and Ginger Rogers are photographed at the Marine Ball. Ginger was a guest at the El Mirador Hotel the year it opened in 1928.

PALM SPRINGS HISTORICAL SOCIETY COLLECTION

BELOW: Frank Bogert with Governor and Mrs. Pat Brown, are shown at the Desert Circus Ball in 1958. The Browns knew Palm Springs well from their many visits, and Governor Brown was instrumental in pushing through legislation that made the Tramway a reality.

PHOTO BY CONRAD HUG

Ray Ryan, owner of the El Mirador Hotel, in 1960 presents Mayor Bogert with a wood-carving he brought back from Africa. *Left to right:* City Council members Johnny Wood, Ruth Hardy, Leonard Wolf, Bogert and Ryan.

PHOTO BY GAIL THOMPSON

RIGHT: The John Guthrie McCallum adobe house was built for him in 1884 by the Indians. The oldest house in the Palm Springs area, it was moved to the Village Green on South Palm Canyon Drive when Pearl and Austin McManus needed room to expand the Oasis Hotel. Today it houses the Palm Springs Historical Society.

PALM SPRINGS HISTORICAL SOCIETY COLLECTION

RIGHT: In 1986, the McCallum Foundation, represented by Leon Parma and Fred Ingram, presented a check for $250,000 to the city as an endowment fund for the Palm Springs Historical Society. The old adobe, home to pioneer Judge John McCallum, is shown behind the group. *Left to right:* Leon Parma; Sally McManus, Director; Elizabeth Coffman Kieley, Chairman of the Historical Society; Fred Ingram; and Councilman Bill Foster.

PALM SPRINGS HISTORICAL SOCIETY COLLECTION

In 1947, Earl Neel, son of pioneer nurseryman C.C. Neel *(at left)*, received the city contract to take out all the existing trees on Palm Canyon Drive and replace them with palms, a proposal originated by City Councilwoman Ruth Hardy. *Inset:* A plaque was placed on one of the trees on October 1, 1949 across the street from The Desert Inn which read, "This mile of palm trees is dedicated to the memory of C.C. Neel by the citizens of Palm Springs in commemoration of his fifty years of loving care of the desert trees and flowers." The plaque has since been removed. Clarence, a popular resident, ran a nursery in the 300 block of North Indian Canyon Drive. Everyone went to him for gardening advice and few people planted a tree or shrub without asking him if that species grew in the desert. Earl Neel, his son, ran Palm Springs' most popular nursery on East Palm Canyon Drive. This photo, taken north of Vista Chino on North Palm Canyon Drive, is a continuation of Clarence Neel's palm tree project.

PHOTO BY GAIL THOMPSON

RIGHT: Roy Fey, a former C.P.A. and builder from Chicago, came to Palm Springs in 1956. During the 1960s, he built more homes and condominiums than any other developer. Most of his projects were in the exclusive Canyon Country Club area. In 1979, he became one of the founders and organizers of the Bank of Palm Springs, serving six years as Chairman of the Board. He was long active in charitable organizations such as the City of Hope, United Way, Jewish Welfare Federation and many others.

PHOTO COURTESY BANK OF PALM SPRINGS

LEFT: Paul DiAmico, one of Palm Springs' most popular citizens, was owner of the DiAmico Steak House on South Palm Canyon Drive, a favorite luncheon spot of the city's leading movers and shakers.

PHOTO COURTESY PAUL DiAMICO

BELOW: *Fantasy Island* star Herve Villechaize and Ginger Rogers at a Marine Ball. *[Eds. Note: Ginger Rogers was a long-time desert resident and lived in Rancho Mirage until her death in 1995.]*

PHOTO BY FRANK BOGERT

ABOVE: Two of the most beautiful women in Palm Springs in 1966 were Helen Dzo Dzo and Barbara Marx. That year, they both served as Desert Circus Queens. Barbara, later Mrs. Frank Sinatra, is one of the valley's hardest and most charming workers. In 1986, she and Frank won the valley's annual award for the most outstanding humanitarians. Barbara Sinatra is also founder-benefactor of The Barbara Sinatra Children's Center, a Rancho Mirage facility founded in 1986 for abused children.

PHOTO BY FRANK BOGERT

ABOVE: Bob Hope and Charles Farrell, two of the city's most famous personalities, pose with O'Donnell Golf Club members Nate Milnor, Jim Kemper and J.E. "Dad" French, the club president.

PHOTO COURTESY PEG RASHALL

LEFT: Leonore Annenberg, president of the Palm Springs Desert Museum in 1972-76, with California Attorney General Evelle Younger and Walter Marks, who was chairman of the fundraising committee for the new museum building and obtained the land from Home Savings and Loan.

PHOTO BY PAUL POSPESIL

RIGHT: The Palm Springs Desert Museum, one of the city's greatest attractions, houses the William Holden Collection and many other interesting exhibits. The world-renowned Armand Hammer and Phillips Collections have both been on exhibition at the museum, which has become one of the most important cultural attractions in the valley.

PHOTO BY MICHAEL DOTSON

ABOVE: Mayor Bogert presents an honorary citizen award to Conrad Adenauer, 88-year-old Chancellor of West Germany. The Lufthansa plane was carrying him on an around-the-world flight in 1960.

PHOTO BY GEORGE AQUINO

BELOW: In 1966, the question of the Chamizal land on the Texas border was settled at a meeting of Lopez Mateos, President of Mexico, and U.S. President Lyndon B. Johnson. Former President Dwight D. Eisenhower, living at Eldorado Country Club at the time, met with the two presidents.

PHOTO BY GEORGE AQUINO

ABOVE: On his last trip to Palm Springs, President John F. Kennedy visited with former President Eisenhower at Eldorado Country Club.

PHOTO BY GEORGE AQUINO

RIGHT: When he was running for Governor of California in 1962, Richard M. Nixon visited Palm Springs. Nixon is shown here talking to Frank Bogert and friends who were heading out on a ride.
PHOTO BY PAUL POSPESIL

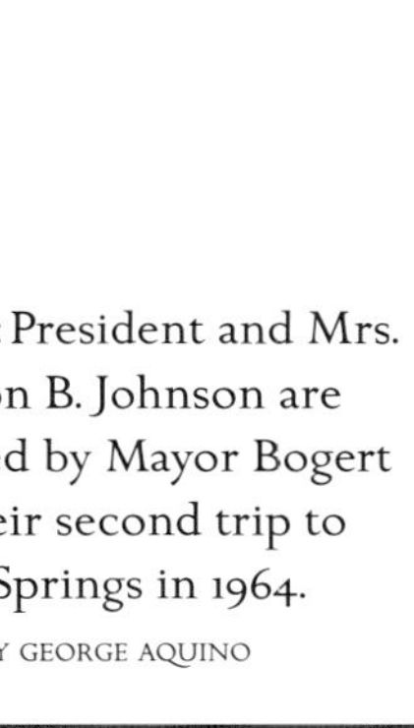

BELOW: President and Mrs. Lyndon B. Johnson are greeted by Mayor Bogert on their second trip to Palm Springs in 1964.
PHOTO BY GEORGE AQUINO

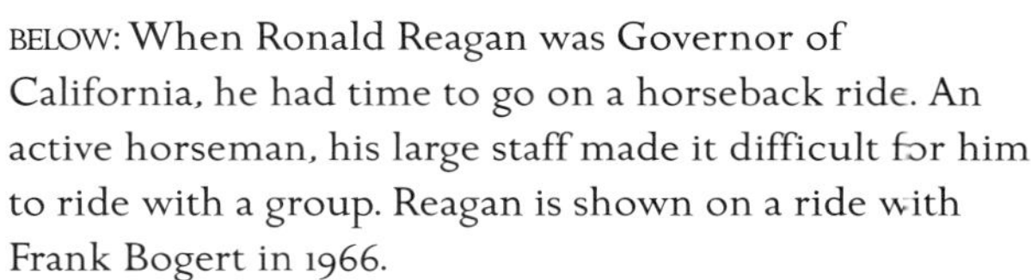

BELOW: When Ronald Reagan was Governor of California, he had time to go on a horseback ride. An active horseman, his large staff made it difficult for him to ride with a group. Reagan is shown on a ride with Frank Bogert in 1966.
PHOTO BY BILL ANDERSON

On a horseback ride into the Indian canyons in 1982 are *(left to right)* Keith Ainsworth from the Coachella Valley Water District; Caspar Weinberger, Secretary of Defense; Boo Hoff of the Desert Riders; William Clark, Jr., Secretary of the Interior; and Frank Bogert, Mayor of Palm Springs. Clark and Weinberger were visiting former Ambassador Annenberg for a New Year's Eve party honoring President Ronald Reagan.

PHOTO BY LAURO NERI

RIGHT: Former House of Representatives Speaker Tip O'Neill came to Palm Springs annually to participate in the Bob Hope Desert Golf Classic. On hand to greet Representative O'Neill is Mayor Frank Bogert.

PHOTO BY PAUL POSPESIL

ABOVE: Mayor Frank Bogert and wife Negie talk with President Reagan at the White House on a 1984 visit to Washington, D.C.

PHOTO BY WHITE HOUSE STAFF

RIGHT: President Reagan and his wife Nancy arrive at Palm Springs Municipal Airport to begin their annual New Year's vacation in the desert. For thirty years, the Reagans stayed at the estate of publisher Walter Annenberg.

PHOTO COURTESY PALM SPRINGS CONVENTION AND VISITORS BUREAU

ABOVE: Mayor and Mrs. Frank Bogert greet California Governor George Deukmejian at the 1983 Governors' Conference in Palm Springs.

PHOTO BY JOHN WESTON

BELOW: President Gerald Ford built a home at Thunderbird Country Club immediately after his retirement from politics. Ford was the honoree at the Americana Ball in 1982, shown with Mayor and Mrs. Bogert.

PHOTO BY ALLEN COOK

ABOVE: Queen Elizabeth and Prince Philip descend the steps of a U.S. presidential plane on their arrival in Palm Springs. En route for a visit to former Ambassador Walter Annenberg's estate in Rancho Mirage, they are greeted by Frank and Negie Bogert, c. 1983.

PHOTO BY STEFANIE SCHLAR

BELOW: Britain's Prince Charles is greeted by Mayor Frank Bogert and his wife Negie on arrival at the Palm Springs Airport in the autumn of 1986. During his weekend stay, the prince played polo and attended a $25,000-a-couple fundraising dinner for Operation Raleigh, a program he founded for young people.

PHOTO BY GARY SHERWIN

Advertisements of the 40s, 50s and 60s captured the spirit of Palm Springs' popular establishments.

Gracious Living in Palm Springs
Invigorating Atmosphere
Ocotillo Lodge
DORIC
OCOTILLO LODGE
Suites — Bungalows — Villas
Aristocratic Cuisine at the Famous Candlewood Room
Phone FAirview 5-2511. 1111 Palm Canyon Drive East-Palm Springs, California
Doric Company also operates: THE MARMONTE . . . SANTA MONICA SURFRIDER INN . . . SANTA BARBARA
THE SAXONY . . . MIAMI BEACH

DON THE
BEACHCOMBER®

del tahquitz
Hotel
Palm Springs ☆ California

"the height of fashion"
NIGHTLY IN THE KOZY
KIVA ROOM
BILLY ALLEN
and his orchestra
TEX KIDWELL
singing troubador
Delightful Dancing Choice Cocktails
IN MAIN DINING ROOM
Superb luncheons from . . $1.85
Complete dinners from . . $4.00
Home of the famous
BAVARIAN BEER FESTIVAL
See you at Palm Springs' Fun Capital
El Mirador
HOTEL

•palm
•springs
•ranch
•club

PALM SPRINGS
Spa
World's most beautiful
Bath House

the O'Donnell Golf Club
PALM SPRINGS
CALIFORNIA

Earl Coffman *(left)* was convinced by Francis Crocker that his dream of a tram to transport people from the valley floor to the top of Mt. San Jacinto could become a reality.

PHOTO COURTESY LANDELLS AVIATION

Palm Springs Aerial Tramway

Sometime in the early 1930s, Francis Crocker, local manager of the California Electric Power Company, began to dream of a tram in Chino Canyon which would transport people to the top of Mt. San Jacinto. He convinced Earl Coffman that it was a distinct possibility. In 1938, Coffman raised enough money from the hotel owners and other local businessmen to finance a preliminary survey. Jim Maynard was enlisted as a guide, and Trav Rogers was hired to establish a camp and provide pack horses in Round Valley. Coffman went to Switzerland and Austria, returning with George Bannerman, an aerial tramway expert.

The survey confirmed that the idea was indeed possible, and Coffman began an earnest effort to make it feasible. With Henry Lockwood as attorney and with the help of Assemblyman Phil Boyd, three bills were passed by the legislature, only to be vetoed by two governors. Governor Earl Warren finally signed the legislation on June 25, 1945, that would establish the Palm Springs Tramway Authority as a public agency and authorize the sale of bonds to pay for the construction of the aerial tramway.

Several hearings took place at which dozens of environmental groups appeared in opposition to the plan. Rights of way had to be secured across Indian land, forest land, Bureau of Land Management land, state parkland and privately-owned land. Culver and Sallie Nichols, who had been involved in efforts to develop the Tramway, donated the land needed for the lower station as well as the right of way for the road.

Lee Kaiser, a San Francisco financier, was brought into the project to work out the sale of bonds. Because of the Korean War and regrouped opposition which made a concerted action to delay the project, bonds were not offered for sale until July 1961. Governor Pat Brown helped considerably with the $7,700,000 bond issue; tax-free revenue bonds paying five and one-half percent became a reality. When the bonds were paid off in thirty-five years, the state would own the project.

When the governing body of the Tramway became a legal authority in 1945, it was called the Mt. San

The mountain station of the Palm Springs Aerial Tramway is shown under construction. The two track cables are each 13,500 feet long.

PHOTO COURTESY LANDELLS AVIATION

Jacinto Winter Park Authority. Governor Warren appointed Leonard Firestone, Swen Wilson, and Jack McKenzie to the Authority; the city of Palm Springs appointed Earl Coffman and Francis Crocker; and Riverside County appointed V. W. Grubbs and James Nusbaum. In 1958, Governor Pat Brown's appointees were Virgil Davidson, Stanley O'Neill and Frank Bogert. The city and county appointments remained the same, with Earl Coffman as chairman.

As soon as the bond sale was assured, Louis deRoll Ironworks from Berne, Switzerland, was engaged. Henri Bodmer from that company drew all the designs for the Tramway. Architects for the valley and mountain stations were from the local firm of Williams, Clark and Frey. Tudor Engineering from San Francisco provided the consulting engineers, and L.E.

Wooden heliport platforms were built during construction of the Tramway at the sites of the four inaccessible towers.

PHOTO COURTESY LANDELLS AVIATION

During the summer of 1938, Trav Rogers packed the first surveyors into Round Valley to lay out the route for the eagerly anticipated tramway. It was completed twenty-five years later in 1963. Shown here are *(left to right)* Francis Crocker, Earle Strebe, Earl Coffman and Trav Rogers. It looks as though the latter three are trying to talk Crocker, a nondrinker, into a little after-dinner toddy. Many villagers drove up the mountain to Idyllwild and hiked to view the site.

PHOTO BY FRANK BOGERT

Dixon and Eric Entman were the general contractors. Albert Webb and Associates surveyed the land; geological and foundation studies were performed by LeRoy Crandall Associates of Los Angeles and Hood and Schmidt, Inc. of Burbank, California.

Construction materials for the five towers and the cables consisted of six hundred tons of steel and over twenty-seven miles of interlocking coil cable, wire rope and strand. They were produced by U.S. Steel's American Steel and Wire Division of Trenton, New Jersey.

Without the use of helicopters, construction would have been impossible. United Helicopters of Santa Monica used five Bell G3s to make 22,000 trips and lift over 5,500 tons of material up the steep cliffs. Heliport platforms were built at the four inaccessible towers.

To those who witnessed the project, construction seemed almost a miracle, although L.E. Dixon, the contractor, and T. T. McKenzie, the resident engineer, made it all appear easy. When it came time to string the two track cables, each 13,500 feet long and weighing 58 tons, a 100-ton hoist was installed at the upper station. A helicopter flew a messenger line over the fourth and fifth towers and heavier lines were added until a cable large enough to pull fifty-eight tons was constructed.

When the Tramway was dedicated on September 12, 1963, eighty people paid one thousand dollars each to be on the first car to the top. Governor Pat Brown and his wife were the first to step out at the top; over 3,500 people followed the governor on that day.

The Palm Springs Aerial Tramway has the longest single lift in the world. Its eighty-passenger cars are also the largest. Paul Zuberbuhler, a Swiss tramway expert who had advised Earl Coffman for many years, proclaimed it the world's most spectacular tramway.

An interesting fact is that you go through five different climate zones from the desert floor at 450 feet to the top of the tram at 8,516 feet. This is equivalent to a trip from Sonora,

Frank Bogert points to a spot in the snow at the top of the tram where a helicopter temporarily got stuck during construction.

PHOTO COURTESY LANDELLS AVIATION

The Palm Springs Aerial Tramway mountain station *(left)* and the valley station *(below)* were designed by the Palm Springs firm of Williams, Clark and Frey.
PHOTO COURTESY LANDELLS AVATION

Mexico, to northern Canada. Riders experience five microclimates from desert to subarctic flora and fauna. There is usually a forty degree temperature difference between the top of the tram and the desert floor.

The Tramway is considered to be one of California's outstanding tourist attractions and one of the valley's greatest assets, attracting hundreds of thousands of visitors annually. No other place in the world can offer winter sunbathing at eighty-five degree temperatures with cross-country skiing only twenty minutes away. When the summer temperatures heat up in the desert, you can escape to cool, spring-like weather in a matter of minutes.

Although Francis Crocker conceived the idea, there were many heroes connected with the Tramway: Earl Coffman, who persevered for twenty-five years with politicians, environmentalists and financiers; Henry Lockwood, who fought the same number of years as legal counsel without pay until the Tramway was completed; L.E. Dixon and T.T. McKenzie who did the impossible in building the project; Don Landells, Joe Dwyer and the other pilots who flew the helicopters; Jimmy Cooper, the first manager; and many others too numerous to mention.

BELOW: The biggest event of the decade was the long-awaited dedication of the Palm Springs Aerial Tramway on Thursday, September 12, 1963. Over four hundred dignitaries, on hand for the first ride, watched Governor Pat Brown cut the ribbon and his wife christen the first car with champagne. Thirty local businessmen paid $1,000 each to ride in the first car with the governor.
PALM SPRINGS HISTORICAL SOCIETY COLLECTION

LEFT: A group of Palm Springs' pioneers at the mountain station of the Aerial Tramway in 1963. *Left to right:* Carl Lykken, sisters Zaddie Bunker and Henrietta Parker, Katherine Finchy and Zaddie's daughter, Frances Bunker Strebe, Willard McKinney and Patricia Moorten.

PALM SPRINGS HISTORICAL SOCIETY COLLECTION

Visitors enjoy riding pack mules in the Mt. San Jacinto wilderness.

PHOTO COURTESY LANDELLS AVATION

RIGHT: Cross-country skiing is popular at the top of the Palm Springs Aerial Tramway. Nearby Hidden Lake, Round Valley and Long Valley boast beautiful ponderosa pines and sweeping vistas of the valley below. Two young skiiers are shown with an unidentified engineer and helicopter pilot/photographer Don Landells *(far right).*

PHOTO COURTESY LANDELLS AVATION

An eighty-passenger car lifts off from the lower station of the Palm Springs Aerial Tramway on the most vertical ascent in the world. In twelve minutes, you rise from 2,400 feet to an 8,500-foot level at the upper station.

PHOTO BY TOM BREWSTER, COURTESY PALM SPRINGS CONVENTION AND VISITORS BUREAU

5

A Desert Playground

Horseback riding was the first outdoor activity available to tourists in Palm Springs. Nearby canyons made popular destinations for riders and hikers. Harriet Cody operated the area's first stable, located on South Palm Canyon Drive near Ramon Road. Two years later, in 1921, Charlie Wise opened another.

When Harriet made a trip to New York a little later, she asked Norman Farra to take over her operation. It was an unfortunate decision for her, as she learned upon her return that Farra had built his own stable on Tachevah Drive and she was out of business. Farra prospered considerably from the many movies being shot in the valley, and at one time owned over two hundred horses and a dozen wagons.

By 1934, there were nine stables in town, among them Earl Proebstel's at Smoke Tree Ranch, Johnny Vance's operation at Deep Well Ranch and Cliff Frager's Desert Inn Stables. Ed Case, Trav Rogers and Lane Sikes each owned stables on Avenida Caballeros next to Tahquitz Drive.

Earl Coffman was the first president of the Desert Riders Club, organized in 1930. Today the club has built hundreds of miles of trails in the surrounding mountains and canyons.

The Field Club was started by a group of horsemen in 1937 on forty acres of land at Sunrise Way and Ramon Road. The Club consisted of a half-mile track, a full-sized polo field and a wood grandstand. For many years the site was used for the Desert Circus, an annual rodeo, hunter trials, national horse shows and harness races. Sunrise Park now occupies that location.

Bill Gilmore, a wealthy steel man from San Francisco who later became one of the owners of Thunderbird Country Club, brought several polo players to the area, including Russ Havenstrite, Bob Skeen, Walt Disney, Bob "Big Boy" Williams and others. Fourteen-goal polo matches were a regular Sunday event. Charlie Farrell often joined in the fun.

Polo had actually been played as early as 1927 on a field that Rod Abbott and Tom Mangin built at Smoke Tree Ranch. It ended with the onset of World War II. Later, Gilmore started indoor polo, a game played in a dirt arena the size of a rodeo ground by a three-man team

---

LEFT: This spectacular view of Mt. San Jacinto at sunrise is seen from Mesquite Country Club which was designed by Bert Stamps in 1984. The course, which is moderately rolling and plays over a long streambed, is open to the public.

PHOTO BY TOM BREWSTER

Desert breakfast rides were always a favorite event for villagers and visitors. This 1941 breakfast was at Smoke Tree Flats. Trav Rogers' two road coaches carried fourteen people each. Others arrived on horseback or by buckboard.

PHOTO BY FRANK BOGERT

with a large, inflatable ball. Six or seven teams were organized for this very popular desert sport.

In 1951, Hank Gogerty, owner of the Desert Air Hotel in Rancho Mirage, turned a beautiful grass runway at his airport into a polo field, and Lyle Nixon and Don Howden started regular polo matches. The Eldorado Polo Club in Indian Wells boasted two fields, a stable and a clubhouse. Today, the latter facility is located on Avenue 50 near Indio. As many as twenty teams with six hundred polo ponies play world-class polo all during the winter season.

Palm Springs and the Coachella Valley remain horse-oriented communities. The Smoke Tree Stable has over one hundred rental horses and thirty boarders. Los Compadres, a private club, keeps thirty boarders. The Vandenburg Equestrian Center in Rancho Mirage has forty boarders, new stables have opened throughout the valley and several quarter horse breeding farms lie in the east end of the valley. The

The National Horse Show at the Field Club in 1940 was a very successful event. Local rider Jimmie Rogers is seen here on her three-gaited Saddlebred.

PHOTO BY FRANK BOGERT, COURTESY JIMMIE ROGERS

The Desert Air Hotel and airport in Rancho Mirage turned part of their grass runway into a polo field *(on the left)*. People flew in from all over the country for lunch and the hotel's famous apple pie. This photo is taken from the air, looking west. Thunderbird Country Club is visible in the distance with Palm Springs at the base of the foothills.

COURTESY CALLAHAN/GOGERTY COLLECTION

McCallum Equestrian Center opened in 1985. The land, donated by ardent horsewoman Pearl McManus, is named in honor of her father. It's the site of the annual Mounted Police Rodeo, the Team Penning Championship and several annual horse shows. *[Eds. Note: That open space property was utilized by the City of Palm Springs for a portion of the second municipal golf course now called Tahquitz Creek Golf Resort.]*

Without a doubt, since the late 1920s, golf has been one of the Coachella Valley's biggest drawing cards. Thousands of homes have been purchased by people seeking both the wonderful winter climate and the wide selection of golf courses. Hotels quickly realized the importance of having access to golf courses for both regular and convention guests.

Prescott Stevens, a far-sighted man, planned for guest activities when he built the El Mirador Hotel. Because he had plenty of land and owned the water company, it was easy for him to build, with the help of Lawrence Crossley, a nine-hole course between Tachevah Drive and Vista Chino. The course, lined with rapid-growing tamarisk trees, opened in 1928 with Mike Flavin as the valley's first golf pro.

El Mirador Hotel owner Prescott Stevens saw to it that there were plenty of activities available for guests. This publicity photo shows visitors enjoying archery, golf and tennis.

PALM SPRINGS HISTORICAL SOCIETY COLLECTION

The stock market crash and subsequent Depression forced Stevens to abandon his course in 1932. His son-in-law, Culver Nichols, moved into the clubhouse, which has been his home ever since. *[Eds. Note: Culver Nichols died in 2001 at age 96.]* From the air, the outline of the fairways can still be seen.

Thomas O'Donnell, a wealthy Desert Inn guest, built a house overlooking the hotel and bought land below the hill to the north. The house was designed by Charles Tanner to match The Desert Inn. After seeing what his friend Stevens had accomplished, O'Donnell decided to build his own nine-hole course. He bought water shares from Stevens for irrigation, and, with the help of George Roberson and John Kline, laid out the course. Guests were allowed to play by invitation only. When his health forced him to give up the game in 1944, he invited twenty-five members to form a club, and he became its first president. The Committee of Twenty-Five exists to this day.

When O'Donnell died in 1945, he left the course to the city with a long-term lease to the

The desert playground atmosphere brought many visitors to Palm Springs and Palm Canyon Drive was bustling during the holidays of the late 1950s.

PALM SPRINGS HISTORICAL SOCIETY COLLECTION

Thomas O'Donnell was a guest at The Desert Inn when he decided to build a house overlooking the hotel and to buy land below the hill to the north where he proceeded with construction on his own nine-hole course in 1927. The view pictured, looking south, is the site of the annual Easter sunrise services.
PALM SPRINGS HISTORICAL SOCIETY COLLECTION

club. J.E. "Dad" French became president; George Howard, the pro; and Larry Sitter, the manager. They arranged for many of the tournaments played on this beautiful course.

Industrialist Floyd Odlum and his wife, famed aviatrix Jackie Cochran, had a ranch in the Indio area. Helen Dettweiler, a well-known golf pro who had flown with Jackie during the war, came to visit in 1945. After driving twenty-four miles each way to play at O'Donnell, Helen and the Odlums decided to build their own golf course. A year later, the 3,091-yard public course, complete with a modern sprinkler system, was built around the Odlum home. With Helen as the pro, the Cochran course became an overnight success.

The Thunderbird Ranch, a dude ranch operation, had been developed at the same time with the idea of selling lots on adjoining land. It was soon obvious to the author, who started the project, that golf would attract more people than a horse-oriented project. Johnny Dawson, a well-known golf promoter, was looking for a location for an eighteen-hole

When Tamarisk Country Club in Rancho Mirage opened in 1952, Ben Hogan, the world's best-known golfer at the time, was hired as the pro. Throughout his career, Hogan claimed a total of sixty-two USPGA titles and amongst major championships, four US Opens, two US Masters, two USPGA Championships and one British Open.
PALM SPRINGS HISTORICAL SOCIETY COLLECTION

This aerial view of Eldorado Country Club shows the fairways nestled in the foothills of the Santa Rosa Mountains shortly after it opened in 1957. The open area at the center of the fairways is where the clubhouse was later built. The Eldorado Polo Club was later located at the site of fields in the lower right.
COURTESY RUSSELL WADE AND CAROL MORTON

course. Barney Hinkle and Tony Burke, two lot salesmen on the ranch, were assigned to contact him. When Johnny was shown the good wells on the property, an agreement was reached.

Arrangements were made to buy eighty additional acres from Ruth Warburton, who owned the adjoining Red Roof Ranch. A corporation with twenty-four stockholders was formed; Lawrence Hughes was hired as golf architect, and Harry Rainville was placed in charge of construction. In 1951, a private golf club opened.

Johnny Dawson became the first president, with the author as manager and Jimmy Hines as the pro. It was one of the first clubs in the country to have lots for sale around the fairways. Among the first buyers were Phil Harris, Bob Hope, Bing Crosby, Leonard Firestone and Hoagy Carmichael.

The following year, Tamarisk Country Club opened for play with Ben Hogan, the world's best-known golfer, as the pro. M.O. Anderson was president, and Charlie Farrell was vice-president. The 7,052-yard course was designed by William Bell, considered to be among the country's greatest golf course architects. It, too, was built with lots available around the fairways, a formula that made possible the development of almost all future courses.

In 1958, a splinter group from Thunderbird, headed by Paul Prom and Desi Arnaz, opened the Indian Wells Country Club. Eddie Susalla, the teaching pro at Thunderbird, became the club manager and pro.

The Bob Hope Classic was originally called the Palm Springs Golf Classic and began in 1960. It was played at Thunderbird, Tamarisk, Indian Wells and Bermuda Dunes Country Clubs. Ben Hogan *(left)* chats with Anson "Bob" Littler, Bob Hope and Monty Moncrief on the course at Thunderbird.

PHOTO BY FRANK BOGERT, PALM SPRINGS HISTORICAL SOCIETY COLLECTION

Lawrence Hughes was course architect for the Eldorado Country Club, built the following year on farmer Jack Page's ranch in the cove next to Indian Wells. Architect Bill Cody's clubhouse was thought to be the ultimate in design.

A group of Chicago investors formed the Westview Development Company and built a course in Palm Springs on a half-section of land they bought from Pearl McManus. Primarily interested in selling lots, the group was delighted to sell the golf course to the city for a very reasonable figure. In 1959, it became the Palm Springs Municipal Golf Course, a very successful business venture for the city. *[Eds. Note: In 1994-95, that open space property was utilized by the City of Palm Springs for a portion of the second municipal golf course, now called Tahquitz Creek Golf Resort.]*

Around this time, an old golf pro, Joe Caldwell, was building a course almost single-handedly. It was a big surprise when he actually opened the Ranch Club course in 1960. The property is now called the Palm Springs Country Club.

Ernie Dunlevie and Ray Ryan started a course so far out of town it was almost in Indio. Named for its high rolling dunes, Bermuda Dunes became one of the valley's most beautiful golf courses.

Seeing a need for another public golf course, the Palm Springs City Council talked Jim Temple into building one. Ever since its opening in 1984, the Mesquite Country Club, on Mesquite Avenue and Farrell Drive, has successfully filled a need for hotel guests who have no golf club affiliation.

The first Bob Hope Classic, one of the most prestigious tournaments in the country, was played in 1960 at Thunderbird, Tamarisk, Indian Wells and Bermuda Dunes courses. Arnold Palmer, the first winner, received $12,000 in prize

Desi Arnaz located his hotel at Indian Wells Country Club. Hole eleven can be seen in the lower left corner.

COURTESY HISTORICAL SOCIETY OF PALM DESERT

One of the valley's major developers, Bill Bone, started by building Deep Well condominiums in 1970 on the site of Frank Bennett's and Phil Boyd's old ranch. Since then, his Sunrise Company has built golf courses and condos throughout the valley as far as La Quinta. His future plans call for billion-dollar developments in the county and in Indian Wells.

PHOTO BY WWW.ARTHURCOLEMAN.COM

money; Cory Pavin won $162,000 in 1987. Over sixteen million dollars have been contributed to charity in the past twenty-seven years from these tournaments. *[Eds. Note: In 2001, the purse had risen to $3.5 million and winner Joe Durant took home $630,000. Nearly $35 million has been contributed to charity in the past forty-three years from these tournaments.]*

For many years, Palm Springs was rightfully known as the winter golf capital of the world. When Rancho Mirage, Palm Desert and Indian Wells were incorporated in the 1970s, the municipalities claimed their own golf courses, and the slogan was no longer appropriate. *[Eds. Note: Though Palm Springs receives most of the publicity, the city can only boast of nine courses within its limits.]*

Over the years, it has been difficult to keep track of the number of country clubs. Bill Bone's Sunrise Company has built several. The Landmark Company, headed by former golf pro Ernie Vossler, bought Mission Hills and built courses at La Quinta as well as five new PGA West courses. Their spectacular Stadium Course is one of the country's most difficult.

The well-regarded Vintage Country Club, the beautiful Morningside, The Springs and Cathedral Canyon Country Club are but a few of the valley's regular, executive and nine-hole courses. No other area can challenge the Coachella Valley as being truly the world's golf capital.

Nothing written about golf in the desert would be complete without mentioning Dinah Shore, a Palm Springs resident for over twenty-five years. She played in numerous tournaments and was the founder of the Dinah Shore Nabisco LPGA Tournament played every spring at Mission Hills Country Club in Rancho Mirage. Through her efforts and promotion the tournament has become one of the largest in the country, equaling the Bob Hope Classic in attendance. *[Eds. Note: Dinah Shore died in 1994, but the tournament she started continues.]*

The first tennis court in the city was at The Desert Inn, although it was used more frequently for outdoor parties than as a tennis court. The El Mirador also built a court beside its large swimming pool.

Dinah Shore with Frank Bogert at a Dinah Shore Tournament gala.

PHOTO BY WWW.ARTHURCOLEMAN.COM

Jose Higueras came from Spain in 1980 to play in a tennis tournament at Mission Hills. At the time, he was the seventh ranked professional in the world. He met a local girl, Donna Bogert, got married in 1982 and made his permanent home in Palm Springs. In 1983, he won the Congoleum ATP Tournament in La Quinta. Now the owner of two ranches and several quarter horses, he is learning to be a cowboy. His Tennis Academy at Mission Hills has become very successful, attracting young players from Europe and other parts of the globe. Jose is a member of the Rancheros Visitadores and Desert Riders and spends his spare time riding with his two children, Jordi and Jenna.
PHOTO COURTESY DONNA HIGUERAS

In 1932, Ralph Bellamy and Charlie Farrell, who rented houses in the village, had a problem getting a hotel court and decided to build their own. Harold Hicks sold them fifty-three acres for $3,500, a reasonable price even for land located in a very windy area.

They planned to build one court, but decided they would have two when they discovered it cost only slightly more. They charged their friends one dollar to use the second court. The following year, they added two more courts, a swimming pool and one room. By 1934, they had built a bar, dining room and high fences around all courts as protection from the wind. Now their club sold $500 memberships. The Racquet Club, a haven for movie stars, producers and tennis buffs, was nationally known by 1938.

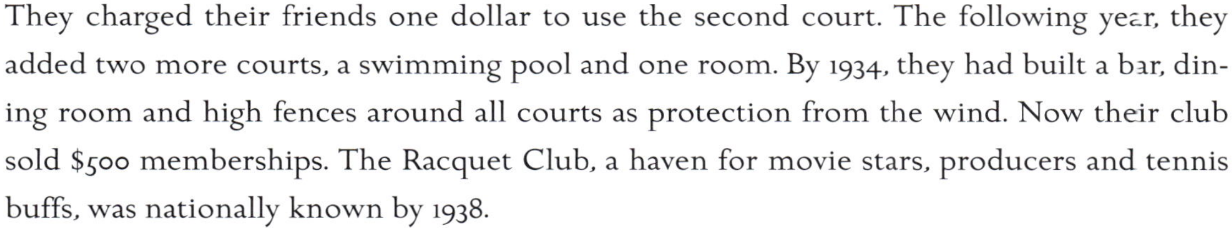

Bill Tilden, Don Budge, Gene Mako, Alice Marble, Eleanor Tennant, Frank Shields, Fred Parry, Jack Kramer and Ted Schroeder were but a few of the famous tennis personalities who played at the Racquet Club.

Following Charlie Farrell's example, two tennis pros who had worked at the Racquet Club negotiated a land lease with Pearl McManus, and they and Pearl designed and built the Tennis Club. It had two tennis courts, a swimming pool and a clubhouse. Within a year, Auntie Pearl foreclosed on their lease and became the sole owner. Over the years, she hired many managers, leased to different people and finally sold the property to Harry Chaddick, a Chicago developer. When he added to the hotel, he added to the tennis facility, ending up with eleven courts.

During the 1970s, when tennis was on the rise in the United States, every hotel, country club, condominium and many private homes built courts. The city had tennis courts at Ruth Hardy Park and added a tennis center on Baristo Road. The Davis Cup tournament was played at the Racquet Club; other tournaments were staged at courts all over the city. For awhile, tennis almost equaled golf in popularity.

La Quinta became a tennis center when Landmark Corporation built its beautiful complex beside the hotel. The stadium was packed each day in 1981 for the Grand Marnier ATP tournament. It was also the site for the 1982, 1983 and 1984 Congoleum tournaments. Jose Higueras, a former Spanish champion and now a Palm Springs resident, won the tournament in 1983. In 1985 and 1986, the renamed Pilot Pen tournament attracted the world's top professionals.

The Eldorado Polo Club on Avenue 50 near Indio has become the winter polo capital. Teams from many foreign countries participate each year in a series of high-goal tournaments. Over six hundred polo ponies are kept on the grounds during the season.

PHOTO BY TOM BREWSTER

Charles Pasarell's huge new tennis center at the Grand Champions resort was the site of the 1987 Pilot Pen tournament. *[Eds. Note: By 2000, the new Indian Wells Tennis Garden, with twenty-two courts and seating for sixteen thousand spectators, was hosting the Tennis Masters Series Indian Wells, which evolved from the Congoleum and Pilot Pen tournaments.]*

Bicycling is probably the valley's third most popular sport. Every city has a network of biking trails. With a few connections, it soon will be possible to ride from Palm Springs to Indio without getting on the main highway.

Ballooning has been a popular sport offered in the eastern valley. For several years, the annual Gordon Bennett Balloon Race drew thousands of spectators to Ruth Hardy Park in Palm Springs.

LEFT: Large settling ponds in the windy area of the San Gorgonio Pass were once a favorite wind surfing site. Smooth water and strong winds contributed to many new speed records. The valley's underground water supply is recharged each year by 240,000-acre-feet of Colorado River water. The windmills in the background are an increasingly important source of energy.

PHOTO BY TOM BREWSTER

RIGHT: Miles of bicycle trails meander throughout Palm Springs.

PHOTO BY WWW.ARTHURCOLEMAN.COM

ABOVE: Clint Eastwood, famous as mayor of Carmel, as well as being a fine actor, participated in the celebrity tournament at the Mission Hills Tennis Center in 1979.

PHOTO BY WWW.ARTHURCOLEMAN.COM

LEFT: Johnny Carson played in the celebrity tournament held each year at La Quinta Tennis Club.

PHOTO BY WWW.ARTHURCOLEMAN.COM

ABOVE: Palm Springs resident Kirk Douglas enjoys time on the courts.

PHOTO BY WWW.ARTHURCOLEMAN.COM

RIGHT: Champion Chris Evert played frequently in the valley.

PHOTO BY WWW.ARTHURCOLEMAN.COM

LEFT: Nancy Lopez has been a frequent player at the Dinah Shore Tournament and won in 1981.

PHOTO BY WWW.ARTHURCOLEMAN.COM

BELOW: Dinah Shore (*left*) presents the 1982 Dinah Shore LPGA Golf Classic winner's trophy to Sally Little at Mission Hills Country Club in Rancho Mirage.

PHOTO BY TOM BREWSTER

LEFT: Jack Lemmon was in Palm Springs in the seventies and eighties playing the Bob Hope Desert Classic.

PHOTO BY TOM BREWSTER

RIGHT: Former Speaker of the House Tip O'Neill at the Bob Hope Desert Classic.

PHOTO BY TOM BREWSTER

LEFT: Bob Hope, host of the Desert Classic.

PHOTO BY TOM BREWSTER

BELOW: Arnie's army followed him to Palm Springs. Arnold Palmer played in Palm Springs often and has won many tournaments, including the first Bob Hope classic in 1960.

PHOTO BY TOM BREWSTER

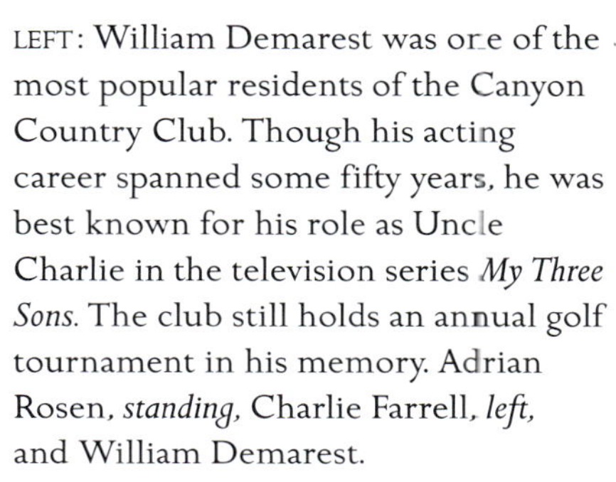

LEFT: William Demarest was one of the most popular residents of the Canyon Country Club. Though his acting career spanned some fifty years, he was best known for his role as Uncle Charlie in the television series *My Three Sons.* The club still holds an annual golf tournament in his memory. Adrian Rosen, *standing,* Charlie Farrell, *left,* and William Demarest.

PALM SPRINGS HISTORICAL SOCIETY COLLECTION

ABOVE: Horseback riders head back to Smoke Tree Stables from the Indian Canyons.

PHOTO BY JACK HOLLINGSWORTH, COURTESY PALM SPRINGS DESERT RESORTS CONVENTION AND VISITORS AUTHORITY

RIGHT: The Gambel's quail are prevalent on the alluvial fans and hills throughout the valley. Often seen within housing projects, they have learned to adapt with civilization's advance.

PHOTO BY GEORGE SERVICE

BELOW: The roadrunner is a favorite desert bird. Visitors find statues, photos and jewelry of him everywhere.

PHOTO BY GEORGE SERVICE

BELOW: The little sidewinder has a peculiar manner of locomotion which gives it its name.

PHOTO BY GEORGE SERVICE

RIGHT: Jean and Ernie Hahn *(left)*, veteran valley residents, were two of the area's hardest workers. Jean has been very active with the Palm Springs Desert Museum, Desert Riders and many charities. Ernie, who built many projects in Palm Springs, developed the Town Center Shopping Mall in Palm Desert. His largest job was to acquire funding for the Bob Hope Cultural Center. They are shown here at the opening of the Hahn Buena Vista Trail with Art Smith and Frank Bogert.

PALM SPRINGS HISTORICAL SOCIETY COLLECTION

BELOW: The coyote, more than any other animal, has learned to coexist with man. They are often spotted in the canyons, and at night may even venture down into the populated areas.

PHOTO BY GEORGE SERVICE

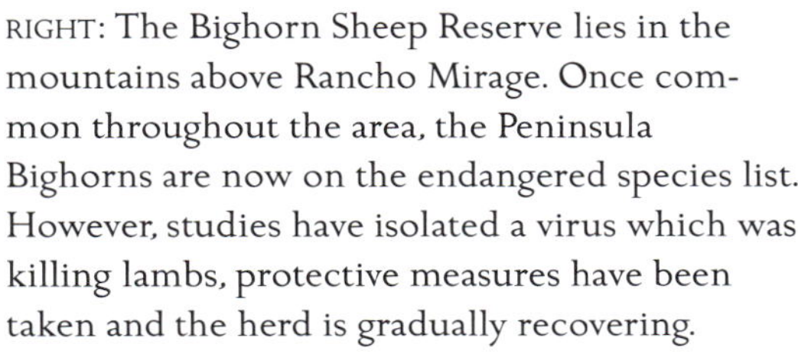

RIGHT: The Bighorn Sheep Reserve lies in the mountains above Rancho Mirage. Once common throughout the area, the Peninsula Bighorns are now on the endangered species list. However, studies have isolated a virus which was killing lambs, protective measures have been taken and the herd is gradually recovering.

PHOTO BY GEORGE SERVICE

ABOVE: Many groups of native palms stand on the eastern side of the valley fed by water diverted to near-surface level by the San Andreas Fault. The Pushawalla palms, shown in the photo, are within the 12,000-acre Coachella Valley Preserve in Thousand Palms. The Preserve is a favorite among valley hikers.

PHOTO BY TOM BREWSTER

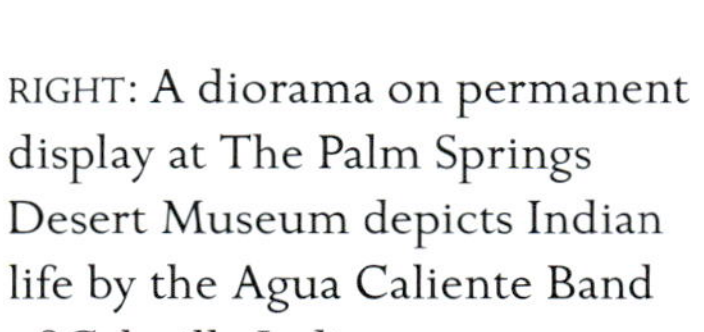

RIGHT: A diorama on permanent display at The Palm Springs Desert Museum depicts Indian life by the Agua Caliente Band of Cahuilla Indians.

PHOTO BY WWW.ARTHURCOLEMAN.COM

Tahquitz Canyon is one of the most beautiful and culturally sensitive areas of the Agua Caliente Reservation. Tahquitz Canyon is home to a spectacular 60-foot waterfall, rock art, ancient irrigation systems, native wildlife and plants. *[Eds. Note: Guided tours are available from the Tahquitz Visitors Center opened in 2000.]*

PHOTO BY TOM BREWSTER

Aerial panorama of Palm Springs and the San Jacinto Mountains in the winter of 1986.

PHOTO COURTESY JOE FLAVIN, MAGIK PICTURES, PALM DESERT

6

The Valley Today

[Eds. Note: This chapter by former Mayor Bogert, written in 1987, reflects the Coachella Valley as it was then. It has been the decision of Mayor Bogert and the editors to leave it essentially unchanged, concluding as it does, the first one hundred years of Palm Springs' history. Updated information appears in the newly written chapter seven, Fifteen Years Later: A Valley Portrait.*]*

For years, nothing but open desert existed between Palm Springs and Indio. A few date, grape and alfalfa ranches sprang up when a plentiful water supply was discovered in underground aquifers. Villages along Highway 111 like Cathedral City, Rancho Mirage, Palm Desert and Indian Wells expanded as locations for new golf courses and subdivisions were sought by developers. By 1982, all of these villages were large enough to incorporate.

Today, the Coachella Valley is composed of nine cities: Desert Hot Springs, Palm Springs, Cathedral City, Rancho Mirage, Palm Desert, Indian Wells, La Quinta, Indio and Coachella. The total permanent population numbers 180,000, with a seasonal rise to approximately 240,000.

Palm Springs can boast of only eight of the valley's sixty-nine golf courses. Its greatest attractions are the Aerial Tramway, Palm Springs Desert Museum, Oasis Water Resort, Moorten Botanical Gardens and the spectacular Indian canyons.

The Palm Springs Municipal Airport, two miles from the center of town, has eight major airlines offering direct service to all parts of the country. Several deluxe hotels have been added to an already fine roster: Maxim's de Paris, Marquis Hotel, Shilo Inn and Palm Springs Plaza. The Riviera Hotel is currently being remodeled, and the Canyon Hotel is adding over two hundred rooms. The Wyndham Hotel and the Palm Springs Convention Center are scheduled to open in early 1988. At that time, Palm Springs will have approximately 7,000 hotel rooms.

Excellent shopping facilities make this "sport" one of the city's greatest assets and one of the main delights for visitors. Shops in the new Desert Fashion Plaza equal those of Rodeo Drive in Beverly Hills. The Courtyard's many boutiques also provide a high-fashion image. Other centers, with more moderately priced merchandise, appeal to local residents.

In addition, excellent art galleries, antique stores and many specialty shops line Palm Canyon Drive. An abundant supply of gourmet restaurants and many quaint eateries

---

LEFT: El Mirador's tower has long been a Palm Springs symbol. Now the site of the Palm Springs Desert Hospital, the tower is preserved as a historical monument. *[Eds. Note: The original tower burned to the ground in 1989. The tower seen today was reconstructed using the original plans.]*

PHOTO BY KIRK OWENS

The soaring roof of the Tramway gas station greets visitors entering Palm Springs on Highway 111. Architect Albert Frey designed the structure with Robson Chambers in 1965. *[Eds. Note: The Tramway gas station was designated a historic site in 1998.]*

PALM SPRINGS HISTORICAL SOCIETY COLLECTION

around town offer choices of Chinese, Japanese, Mexican, Italian and other types of cuisine.

Baseball fans have an opportunity to watch a game when Gene Autry's California Angels return to the desert for spring practice and exhibition games. Angels Stadium is open all summer, and the Palm Springs Angels play nightly games with other farm-league teams.

Desert Hot Springs, six miles north of Palm Springs, has many spas, several small hotels and a number of fine restaurants. Cabot's Old Indian Pueblo Museum gives tourists a glimpse of life in early America, and the Mission Lakes Country Club offers an excellent golf course.

Cathedral City, bordering Palm Springs to the east, is the home of the Desert Princess Hotel and Golf Course, Cathedral Canyon Country Club and an adjoining hotel as well as several smaller hotels and restaurants.

Palm Springs residents and visitors alike enjoy the welcoming sight of the *Palm Springs* sign at the northern entrance to town.

PHOTO BY WWW.ARTHURCOLEMAN.COM

Next is Rancho Mirage, a city that got its start with two golf courses, Thunderbird and Tamarisk, and now has eleven courses and plenty of land available for more development. The city's two largest hotels are Mission Hills Resort and Marriott's Rancho Las Palmas Resort. A beautiful new Ritz-Carlton hotel, under construction in the hills overlooking the city, will open in 1988. Many fine restaurants are located in Rancho Mirage on "Restaurant Row" along Highway 111.

The Eisenhower Medical Center, Betty Ford Center for Chemical Abuse, Barbara Sinatra Center for Abused

Children and Annenberg Center for Health Sciences are Rancho Mirage's most outstanding achievements. The city is also home to Frank Sinatra and Ambassador Walter Annenberg, whose estate includes a private golf course. The Bighorn Sheep Reserve lies in the hills south of town.

Palm Desert, to the east, is one of the valley's fastest-growing cities. College of the Desert, a community college, was built in this location because the city is geographically in the center of the valley. The new and tremendously successful Town Center, built by Ernie Hahn, includes an ice skating rink and many fine shops. El Paseo, too, has become a fine street for upscale shopping.

The Bob Hope Cultural Center, which will include the McCallum Theatre and several smaller theaters, opens in 1988. At that time, the valley will finally have proper facilities for staging operas, ballets and other theatrical events.

A major tourist attraction, The Living Desert, was established by the first mayor of Palm Springs, Philip Boyd.

Palm Desert has nineteen golf courses, more than any other city in the valley. With so much undeveloped land still available, more spectacular courses are already on the drawing board for the near future. The city's largest hotel is Marriott's Desert Springs Resort, with 900 rooms, two complete eighteen hole golf courses and superb convention facilities. Several smaller hotels and many excellent dining spots round out the visitor attractions.

Indian Wells started with Eldorado Country Club and Indian Wells Country Club. There are now six golf courses. Among the major hotels are Erawan Garden Hotel, Ramada Inn and the exclusive Grand Champions Resort. The latter resort also contains a 10,000-seat tennis

ABOVE & BELOW: The Palm Springs Aerial Tramway offers winter sports, miles of hiking trails and a refreshing break from the heat in the summer. The view from the top is breathtaking.
PHOTOS BY TOM BREWSTER

Chester "Cactus Slim" Moorten and his wife Patricia founded Moorten Botanical Garden on South Palm Canyon Drive in 1938. This historic landmark is spread out over one and a half acres and consists of more than 3,000 different varieties of desert plants from around the world. Among the major deserts of the Southwest represented here are the Mojave, Sonoran and Baja. The Moortens' son, Clark, now runs the garden.

PHOTO BY TOM BREWSTER, COURTESY PALM SPRINGS DESERT RESEORTS CONVENTION AND VISITORS AUTHORITY

stadium that has been the site of the annual Pilot Pen Tennis Tournament. A new 192-room Stouffer Hotel will open in 1988. The Indian Wells Racquet Club is located on the site of the old Indian well that gave the town its name.

In a beautiful cove next to Indian Wells lies the city of La Quinta. A charming Spanish hotel, built in 1921, has been a famous resort for many years. Today, the area is popular for its eight golf courses, four of which make up PGA West, where a fifth is under construction. From La Quinta, fine riding and hiking trails lead into the nearby hills and a palm-lined canyon.

Indio, the valley's oldest city, was incorporated in 1930. Its main thrust was farming and industry. It is also the location of the county's Superior Court and Planning Department. Many date-packing sheds are found here as the area raises most of the valley's produce. The Coachella Valley's average date yield of $5,000 per irrigated acre is the highest in the world.

Indio is now looking forward to becoming a tourist destination in its own right. Three golf courses have already been built and several new projects are in the planning stages.

The ninth city, at the southern end of the valley, is Coachella. Like Indio, it has been an industrial and agricultural center, but is now actively seeking a future as a resort area.

Large developers from other parts of the world tell us that the valley is only in its infancy. Local developers, such as Bill Bone and John Wessman, agree. It is predicted that by the year 2000 the valley will have a population of over 400,000.

Palm Canyon Drive is a shopping paradise. The thoroughfare is lined with fine boutiques, specialty stores, antique shops and galleries.

PHOTO BY TOM BREWSTER, COURTESY PALM SPRINGS DESERT RESORTS CONVENTION AND VISITORS AUTHORITY

The Palm Springs Convention Center is one of the most unique convention facilities in the country, hosting conventions, exhibitions, and trade shows. Located on Avenida Caballeros, it is just three blocks east of downtown and a half mile west of the airport. Built in 1986, it adjoins the Wyndham Hotel. Here, the Tahquitz witch is seen looming over the city.

PHOTO BY WWW.ARTHURCOLEMAN.COM

Several of the valley's golf courses and large developments, such as Palm Desert Resort and Bermuda Dunes, are still part of the county, although most of them lie within the sphere of influence of future cities. A need to maintain open space will certainly require the construction of additional golf courses.

One hundred years ago, John Guthrie McCallum and his partners held a land auction, selling lots for forty-five dollars. Today, many of those same lots are valued at more than $700,000. McCallum spent a fortune building nineteen miles of rock-lined ditches to bring water to Palm Springs, little dreaming that he was sitting on top of a basin with millions of gallons of water in underground aquifers. Many of the valley's over three thousand wells could individually pump twice the amount of water his ditch could carry.

When Nellie Coffman built the cement-reinforced lobby and dining room at The Desert Inn, she said, "This building will be here one hundred years from now." Today, however, the Desert Fashion Plaza and six-story Maxim's Hotel stand on the site.

All valley cities are studying their master plans in an attempt to control growth. Densities are being cut back, buildings are limited to six stories with proper setbacks, hillside projects are extremely limited and open space ordinances are being put into effect. While it is inevitable that the valley will grow, it will certainly not lose its charm.

Plans are underway to solve the traffic problem. Many new bridges and cross streets leading to the interstate freeway have been added. The new parkway on Dinah Shore Drive will become a reality within the next few years.

With the mutual efforts of all nine cities working together on proper planning, the Coachella Valley surely will retain its character as a unique resort destination.

Palm Springs City Hall is an especially fine structure in the modernist tradition of innovative civic architecture, perfectly adapted to its site and climate. The barrel-shaped sun screens along the front make the building cool and inviting on even the sunniest days. It was first designed in 1952 by architect Albert Frey. John Porter Clark, Robson Chambers and Stewart Williams made later additions.

Above: PHOTO BY TOM BREWSTER

Right: PALM SPRINGS HISTORICAL SOCIETY COLLECTION

The beautiful fountain at Palm Springs' airport was created and designed by Julio de la Peña, one of Mexico's greatest architects. Donated by Pearl McManus, it is one of the few things in the valley to bear her name rather than that of her father, John Guthrie McCallum. The fountain's dedication took place on April 2, 1968, shortly after Pearl's death. Weighing over 40 tons, its 398 pieces were handmade from cantera stone from Degollado, Jalisco, Mexico. The fountain sprays eight hundred gallons of water at a time.

PHOTO COURTESY PALM SPRINGS INTERNATIONAL AIRPORT

City Council and staff in 1987. *Left to right:* Dick Smith, City Manager Norm King, Secretary Mary T. Martin, Mayor Frank M. Bogert, Sharon Apfelbaum, Eli Birer and Bill Foster. Mary Martin served the mayor and city manager for over twenty years.

PHOTO BY SCOTT MILIMAN

Howard Wiefels, former mayor of Palm Springs (1967-1974), represents the family of Wiefels and Son Funeral Directors. The business was founded in Banning in 1908, with the Palm Springs location opening in 1948.

PHOTO COURTESY LORI WIEFELS MATTHEWS & MICHAEL WIEFELS

ABOVE: The Agua Caliente Band of Cahuilla Indians controls 32,000 acres of land in and around Palm Springs. During Richard Milanovich's tenure as Tribal Chairman, the relationship between the Indians and the city has been the best in its history. Together the Indians and the city can claim many major accomplishments.

Above: PALM SPRINGS HISTORICAL SOCIETY COLLECTION

Upper left: PHOTO BY WWW.ARTHURCOLEMAN.COM

The Delgado family is Palm Springs' greatest success story. Florencio and Maria started a small Mexican restaurant on North Palm Canyon Drive in 1958. The family owns two Las Casuelas restaurants in Palm Springs, Las Casuelas Nuevas in Rancho Mirage and have plans for additional restaurants. Their children, Patricia, Florence, Joaquin and Robert, together with their families, operate the properties. Without a doubt, they are the most popular and successful restaurants in the valley, doing a multi-million-dollar business annually.

PHOTO COURTESY THE DELGADO FAMILY

BELOW: Las Casuelas Terraza, one of the Delgado family restaurants is located on South Palm Canyon Drive. *[Eds. Note: This photo shows the restaurant after remodeling in 2001.]*

PHOTO BY WWW.ARTHURCOLEMAN.COM

Maria and Florencio Delgado in the original Las Casuelas. *[Eds. note: Florencio died in 1992.]*

PHOTO COURTESY THE DELGADO FAMILY

ABOVE: Barbara Sinatra is one of the valley's most prominent charity fundraisers. Her main interest is the Barbara Sinatra Children's Center at Eisenhower Medical Center. Polo matches and many other events are held annually to support her center for abused children.

PHOTO BY WWW.ARTHURCOLEMAN.COM

LEFT: Frank Sinatra has been a valley citizen for almost fifty years. *[Eds. Note: Sinatra died in May, 1998.]* For many years he had a home in Palm Springs. In the 1950s, he built a large estate on the fairway at Tamarisk Country Club in Rancho Mirage. The money he raised and donated to the Desert Hospital, Eisenhower Medical Center and hundreds of other worthy charities would amount to several million dollars. No one has done more for the valley than "Old Blue Eyes."

PHOTO BY TOM BREWSTER

RIGHT: Jim Temple, developer of the Mesquite Country Club and over 1,500 condominium units in Palm Springs is shown with his family. Wife Phyllis does all the decorating for his projects; son Mark handles the construction; and daughter Laura, a real estate broker, is in charge of all sales. Another daughter, Valerie, and husband, Doug McCallum, run their cattle ranch in Montana. The entire family forms the Temple off-road racing team and participates in numerous races in Mexico and the southwest.

PHOTO BY FRANK BOGERT

Bill Holden, one of Hollywood's most loved actors, made his home in Palm Springs. He was a partner with Ray Ryan in many projects, including the Mt. Kenya Safari Club. He lived in Deep Well for many years and moved into his new house in Southridge shortly before his untimely death. Holden left his entire African and Asian collection, valued at several million dollars, to the Palm Springs Desert Museum.

PHOTO BY WWW.ARTHURCOLEMAN.COM

BELOW: Alice Faye, wife of Phil Harris, was one of Hollywood's most glamorous and beautiful movie stars. She was also a true desert pioneer, being one of the first members of Charlie Farrell's Racquet Club and an active participant in most valley events. Their two daughters, Phyllis and Alice, were raised in the area.

PHOTO BY BRIAN MAURER

ABOVE: Phil Harris, a longtime desert resident, built the first house at Thunderbird Country Club. His many personal appearances for charitable parties and golf tournaments made him one of the valley's most venerated performers.

PHOTO BY WWW.ARTHURCOLEMAN.COM

LEFT: Frank Bogert and his three daughters. *Left to right:* Donna Higueras, Denni Russell and Cindy Lamm.

PHOTO BY PAUL POSPESIL

BELOW: Milton Jones, has published *Palm Springs Life* since 1965. Also owner of the magazine, Jones has made the publication one of the best metropolitan magazines in the country, consistently ranking in the top ten nationwide. Its fine color photography and exclusive coverage have been a tremendous asset to Palm Springs and the entire valley.

PHOTO COURTESY PALM SPRINGS LIFE

ABOVE: John Wessman, a valley developer and builder for decades, has built several regional shopping centers, office buildings and residential subdivisions. The architecture of most of his buildings, like the beautiful Plaza del Sol, seen behind him, reflects its Mexican heritage. Columns, walks, doors and window frames are all made from cantera stone imported from Jalisco, Mexico.

PHOTO BY FRANK BOGERT

BELOW: Former President Gerald Ford and his wife Betty built a home on Thunderbird Golf Course as soon as he retired from politics. The President, who has played in every major golf tournament, also became involved in many valley projects. Betty Ford is active in various charitable groups. She started the Betty Ford Center for Substance Abuse in Rancho Mirage, a tremendously worthwhile resource known all over the world.

PHOTO COURTESY PRESIDENT GERALD FORD

ABOVE: From the 1950s Gene Autry lived in Palm Springs. His home was in the center of the Gene Autry Hotel grounds. Jackie, his wife, was raised in Palm Springs. At the time of their marriage she was vice president of a local bank. The Autrys have been active in all phases of city life. Until they moved to Arizona, spring practice of Autry's California Angels team was one of Palm Springs' major attractions. The Autrys generously supported the Eisenhower Medical Center, Desert Hospital, Palm Springs Senior Center and many additional charitable organizations. In 1987, they were recipients of the Coachella Valley Humanitarian Award. Jackie spends much of her time working with the Gene Autry Western Heritage Museum in Los Angeles. The museum contains the world's largest collection of western memorabilia. *[Eds. Note: In 2001, she became president of baseball's American League.]* Today, Gene is even more of a legend than he was during his long career in the film and recording industries. He is credited with ninety-three films and over two thousand records, including nine gold and one platinum. *[Eds. Note: Gene Autry died in 1998.]*

PHOTO COURTESY GENE AND JACKIE AUTRY

LEFT: Jim and Jackie Lee Houston were desert visitors for many years before they made Palm Springs their home in 1975. Jackie Lee owns and operates Desert Television, a CBS affiliate and KPSP, a local radio station. Energetic philanthropists, they organize and sponsor numerous charitable events and give to many more, including Angel View Crippled Children's Foundation, Animal Samaritans and the McCallum Theatre.

PHOTO COURTESY JIM AND JACKIE LEE HOUSTON

7

Fifteen Years Later: A Valley Portrait

Since this chronicle was published fifteen years ago, change and growth have accelerated. Some of the Palm Springs hotels mentioned in the previous chapter have undergone name changes; specifically, Maxim's de Paris is currently the Hyatt Regency Suites and the Palm Springs Plaza is the Palm Springs Hilton Resort. The Canyon Hotel was demolished several years ago. An important development during the 1990s was the resurgence of older, small hotels, many dating from the 1930s and 40s, once again attractively furnished and contributing significantly to Palm Springs' tourism-based economy.

The "new" Desert Fashion Plaza never lived up to expectations and was sold, several times. Under new owners, it is expected to emerge in the next few years entirely redesigned and focused upon the city's developing emphasis on its "village" heritage, as well as upon entertainment and shopping. The Courtyard is now primarily a theater and office complex. After suffering through the economic doldrums of the late eighties and early nineties, Palm Canyon Drive, north to south, is undergoing a facelift. Shops, hotels, restaurants and theaters are humming with new vitality.

Gene Autry's California Angels decamped to Mesa, Arizona, and the stadium, renamed Palm Springs Stadium, is used primarily by local kids' sports teams.

The legalization of Indian gaming has greatly stimulated the economy: In 1996, the Agua Caliente Band opened its first casino, the Spa Resort Casino, built in and around the palms and springs where Palm Springs began. Instant success led, in early 2001, to the seventy-million-dollar sister operation, the Agua Caliente Casino in Rancho Mirage. Both casinos are financed and operated solely by the Tribe. The Twentynine Palms and Cabazon bands each have successful casinos in the area.

With growth and a healthy economy, the cultural life of the Coachella Valley is flourishing. In 1996, The Palm Springs Desert Museum added to its beautiful building the 20,000

LEFT: This homage to Palm Springs' Indian heritage, entitled *Agua Caliente Women*, by Doug Hyde, was one of the first art works (1994) erected by the city's Public Arts Commission. It is prominently located on the Tahquitz Canyon Way median across from the Spa Resort and Casino.

PHOTO BY WWW.ARTHURCOLEMAN.COM

Thursday evenings in Palm Springs can be leisurely spent strolling along Palm Canyon Drive enjoying the Village Fest. Original artwork, crafts and jewelry share the stage with fruit, vegetable and flower stands as well as food vendors. The weekly event was initiated in 1991 by the City Council and City of Palm Springs Department of Parks, Recreation and Facilities.

PHOTO BY WWW.ARTHURCOLEMAN.COM

square-foot Steve Chase Wing, making the museum now the largest between Los Angeles and Phoenix. Palm Springs architect Stewart Williams designed both the handsome original building and the new wing. The museum collects Agua Caliente and other Indian artifacts as well as contemporary art. Its Annenberg Theater brings a rich variety of cultural offerings to the area, as do the larger McCallum Theatre in Palm Desert and the restored Palm Springs High School auditorium.

The Agua Caliente Indians operate an informative and attractive museum on the Village Green, along with its neighbors, the Palm Springs Historical Society and Ruddy's General Store museums. The Palm Springs Public Library in Sunrise Park also collects and preserves local history. It is the oldest and largest library in the Coachella Valley with nearly 200,000 volumes. Many other local libraries and historical societies now enhance, protect and promote the culture and history of the valley. The Children's Discovery Museum opened recently in Rancho Mirage, and an invaluable collection of twenty-seven, air-worthy World War II planes forms the backbone of the fine Palm Springs Air Museum. Included is a B-17, one of eleven still flying. The museum's volunteers are mostly pilots who flew similar craft in combat. Founded in 1996, over 100,000 people visit yearly. Palm Desert's The Living Desert, begun with a lone, injured kit fox, now has 470 animals of 158 different breeds and hundreds of varieties of flora in 1,400 acres. In the year 2000, the popular family attraction had 325,000 visitors, shepherded by 450 volunteers.

The Spa Resort Casino was added to the Spa Hotel complex in 1995 and is situated on nine acres in the heart of downtown Palm Springs. The casino is owned and operated by the Agua Caliente Band of Cahuilla Indians, which has also opened the Agua Caliente Casino on Bob Hope Drive in Rancho Mirage. Expansion of the Palm Springs casino will soon be underway.

PHOTO BY TOM BREWSTER, COURTESY PALM SPRINGS DESERT RESORTS CONVENTION AND VISITORS AUTHORITY

The Village Green Heritage Center offers a glimpse into pioneer life in Palm Springs. The Palm Springs Historical Society makes its home in the McCallum Adobe, which was built in 1884 and is today the oldest remaining building in the area. The other antique-filled structure, operated by the Historical Society, is Miss Cornelia White's House, partially built in 1893 with railroad ties by the city's first hotel owner, Dr. Welwood Murray. Also at the center are Ruddy's General Store and the Agua Caliente Cultural Museum. All are open to the public.

PHOTO BY TOM BREWSTER, COURTESY PALM SPRINGS DESERT RESORTS CONVENTION AND VISITORS AUTHORITY

During the 1990s, houses and some commercial buildings designed during the 1950s and 1960s by Modernist or International-style architects were rediscovered by aficionados. These post-war buildings, emphasizing clean, horizontal lines and the use of natural materials such as steel, concrete, glass and wood, are being restored with careful attention to period details and are at the center of a Palm Springs renaissance. The city boasts one of the largest single concentrations of mid-century buildings in the world, and they have been written about and photographed by travel, style, art and architecture writers worldwide. Thousands of visitors come to Palm Springs to view these creations by Richard Neutra, Albert Frey, Donald Wexler, Stewart Williams, William Cody, William Krisel and others.

In 1990, then-Mayor Sonny Bono founded the Nortel Networks Palm Springs International Film Festival. Originally attracting a majority of local fans, the Festival now offers an important venue for connecting potential distributors and filmmakers and is another major, international attraction. New, smaller festivals are offering their own followers a veritable feast of attractions.

The Palm Springs Follies, a polished variety show starring old-time headliners, keeps the historic Plaza Theater perpetually packed. Tour groups come from hundreds of miles to see the glamorous "long-legged lovelies" perform their Las Vegas-style revues.

Throughout the Coachella Valley, growth statistics click upward hourly: 330,000 full-time residents are now in the valley; in season, with visitors and second homeowners, over

The "Legendary Line of Long-Legged Lovelies", aged 50-85, are a trademark of the *Fabulous Palm Springs Follies*, founded in 1991 by Riff Markowitz. He continues as the impresario of the vaudeville-style show held in the historic Plaza Theater. By the end of the 2002 season, attendance had topped two million.

PHOTO BY WWW.ARTHURCOLEMAN.COM

Palm Springs International Airport is owned by the City of Palm Springs and operated by the Department of Aviation. It serves the entire Coachella Valley and meets the challenge of a booming convention and tourism based economy. Among its amenities are a golf and tennis pro shop, a natural grass putting green, an airport business center and a play structure for children. Originally designed by Donald Wexler in 1964, the new terminal, designed by Gensler Architects and opened in 1999, was a component of the 1994 airport master plan.

PHOTO BY WWW.ARTHURCOLEMAN.COM

500,000. There are more than 30,000 swimming pools; upwards of 600 tennis courts; and 14,763 rooms in 233 hotels – an array of choices for vacations or conventions.

There are a phenomenal 109 golf courses in the Coachella Valley, nine of which are in Palm Springs. Usually two or three are under construction. Forty-two hundred windmills, one of the world's largest concentrations, stand tall in the desert mouth of San Gorgonio Pass, spinning out electricity.

Nearly every facet of the Palm Springs Airport has been greatly expanded and modernized to twenty-first century standards. Serving more than one million passengers yearly, and now virtually in the city's center, the handsome airport has added a confident "International" to its name.

The Santa Rosa and San Jacinto Mountains National Monument, created by a bill proposed by Representative Mary Bono, was passed into law in 2001. Containing 272,000 acres of the valley's watershed from the mountain rims to the limits of the cities, it extends from San Gorgonio Pass on the northwest to the Martinez Canyon in the southeast.

As in Palm Springs, everywhere in the valley there is action. Cathedral City has bulldozed its core area to build an ambitious new civic center. Plans for the city include theaters, restaurants and upscale hotels. In 2000, the 16,000-seat Indian Wells Tennis Garden, which replaced the Hyatt Grand Champions courts, opened for world-class tournaments and major concerts. In La Quinta, the annual Arts Festival has grown from the work of only a

Conceived in 1990 by Mayor Sonny Bono The Palm Springs International Film Festival now produces two world-class international film events. The Nortel Networks Palm Springs International Film Festival is held in January and the Palm Springs International Festival of Short Films follows in August. The Camelot Theater on Baristo Road near Farrell Drive was purchased by Ric and Rozene Supple to serve as home base to these festivals. The Supples are prominent media owners and philanthropists.

PHOTO COURTESY PALM SPRINGS INTERNATIONAL FILM FESTIVAL

handful of artists to one of the pre-eminent adjudicated shows in the nation. Some 250 artists gross more than two million dollars each year, and the show has graduated to its own twenty-eight acre site. Profits go to arts education.

The Eldorado and Empire Polo Clubs have combined to form a giant polo center with more than three thousand ponies standing in the Indio area during the season. Nearby, HITS (Horse Shows In The Sun) has developed a show-jumping arena attracting top horses and riders in international circuit competition.

Del Webb's retirement community, Sun City, opened in 1991 in Palm Desert. It now has 3,500 homes and 3,000 residents. The College of the Desert strains at the seams, and in 2002 a new California State University branch campus is opening in Palm Desert, which has also become the valley's retail center. Rancho Mirage recently opened "The River," an astonishing new retail and entertainment center.

Increasingly popular as alternative sources of energy, wind turbine generators produce electricity by harnessing the wind. Wind turbine generators require average wind speeds of at least 21 km/h (13 mph). The largest of these windmills stands 150 feet tall. The compartments at the top containing the generator, hub and gearbox weigh 30,000 to 45,000 pounds. A wind turbine can produce 300 kilowatts an hour – the amount of electricity used by a typical household in a month.

PHOTO BY WWW.ARTHURCOLEMAN.COM

ABOVE: The Resort Course at the Tahquitz Creek Golf Resort in Palm Springs was designed by well-known architect Ted Robinson in 1995. Open to the public, it is a desert links style course with rolling terrain, well placed bunkers, wonderful waterscapes and tremendous mountain views. The course is managed by the City of Palm Springs Department of Parks, Recreation and Facilities and is built on land which was formerly part of the McCallum Equestrian Center, donated by Pearl McManus.

PHOTO BY WWW.ARTHURCOLEMAN.COM

LEFT: The "Playground of Presidents" title still holds true for the Coachella Valley. In 1995 former Presidents George Bush and Gerald Ford as well as President Bill Clinton enjoy golf at Indian Wells Country Club.

PHOTO BY WWW.ARTHURCOLEMAN.COM

The Palm Springs Desert Museum features art, natural science and the performing arts. Set at the base of Mt. San Jacinto in the heart of downtown Palm Springs, the Museum's outstanding architecture is in harmony with its desert surroundings, offering spacious galleries, sculpture gardens, a lecture hall and the 433-seat Annenberg Theater.

PHOTO BY WWW.ARTHURCOLEMAN.COM

For more than half of the first one hundred years of our modern history, a rider in the Palm Springs foothills would have looked down on a true oasis – a green dot on a sand sea. No longer. The City of Palm Springs and its neighbors are built upon that sand which is now landscaped, mile after mile, lush and lovely. Sand is fast disappearing as buildings hug the waterline of the old desert lake and fill the alluvial fans where the canyons flare.

Golf courses are meadows between the long reaches of palm shade, oleander hedges, and bougainvillea-covered walls. We've turned the shoulder of the Santa Rosas now – spreading still.

Frank Bogert and Ray Corliss
October, 2002

PHOTO BY GEORGE SERVICE

Personality Index

D

E

F

G

H

I

J

K

L

M

N

O

P

R

S

T

U

V

W

Y

Z